LORD OF THE DAWN

Quetzalcoatl

The Plumed Serpent of Mexico

Written and Illustrated
by
Tony Shearer

Paper Edition   ISBN 0-911010-74-2
Cloth Edition   ISBN 0-911010-99-8

Published by Naturegraph Publishers, Inc., Happy Camp,
California 96039

"For My Children:
Mark, Dena, Gina,
Tony, Anita

AND

For the Old Smoke
At Charm Springs
on
Bald Mountain"

ACKNOWLEDGMENTS

To Dr. Alfonso Caso, and the University of Oklahoma Press, thanks for permission to quote from their book, AZTECS; PEOPLE OF THE SUN, as quoted on pages 146, 147 and 175 in this book.

Rhea Vose for her help with the manuscript. Vinson and Barbara Brown for their patience and faith.

And the following for their time, wisdom, patience and understanding; Helen and Tony Maliszewski; Henry Crowdog; Richard Tallbull; Ruth Underhill; Hugh B. Terry; Ken Slagle; Marie Wormington; Pro. Castulo Romero; Howard Leigh; and my sister Irene Allander who walks the Bright Path. . .

Many thanks

FOREWORD

By Vinson Brown

Out of formlessness form was created. Out of dark nothingness light and beauty were created. Out of single atoms complex molecules eventually came into being from which life was created. Now we look at a rainbow or a waterfall tossing down over mighty cliffs and we see that beauty. A tree traces its loveliness against a blue sky in springtime, or a girl's laughter tinkles from the playing field and we become aware of beauty. Was all this beauty, all this intricate form and these marvelous patterns of life, of minerals, of liquids, of gases, created by blind impulse or was there a Creator and did He have a plan?

In this book I believe we see a part of this great plan! In the veins of Tony Shearer, the author of this book, there courses the blood of the American Indian (the Sioux). He went to ancient Mexico to find and study the source of American Indian culture and civilization. Sitting at the feet of the great archaeologists, like Wormington and Caso, and working with them, reading everything he could find written about those fantastic civilizations and Middle America, his mind became filled with myriads of facts. He could easily have written a strictly factual book about ancient Mexico, but there are many such factual books, several of them very fine. Yet Tony wanted to catch something in a book of probably more vital importance, the Spirit of a People and the whole meaning of their lives on this planet! So the Blood of the Indian within him led him, as does the arm and hand of the fine bowman drive the arrow, unerringly to the heart of a great spiritual adventure. This is an adventure that you can follow too and find the meanings behind the rainbow and the morning star, the ghost path of the Milky Way, and the carvings of an ancient and vanished civilization whose prophetic dreams and warnings may come to us just in time to save our world from a destruction and degradation too horrible to imagine.

INTRODUCTION

This is a love story, and its history lies deep in the heart of Ancient America. The story is set within the framework of a terrible and yet wonderful prophecy, the Prophecy of the Thirteen Heavens and the Nine Hells. This prophecy was carved on the rocks of the sacred city of Palenque in southern Mexico more than fifteen hundred years ago. Carved in glyphs and based on intricate mathematical calculations, it called for the near to utter destruction of all things in Indian America, but promised a fantastically beautiful and harmonious New World for those who kept the covenant with the Creator and the Earth Mother:

Thus: *"All things that must be*
must be in balance,
And -- that takes practice."

The Little People (Pockwatchies and Tlaloques) spoken of in this book, are not to be confused with the elves or fairies of Ireland (though there may be a relationship we do not understand). But the Pockwatchies and Tlaloques to the ancient people of southern Mexico, were believed to be the servants of the Rain God (Tlaloc). Thus, the Indians believed the Little People were the appointed Guardians of the Earth Mother and the first inhabitants of the First Creation. And, like the Prophecy, they too have their own history and reason for being.

If you ask, "are they real, do they actually exist?" I will answer, yes, in the minds of the Ancient Americans they not only existed on this Earth, but also in the Rain Paradise of another world. The Indians believed them to be less than three inches tall, but extremely powerful, for they could bring rain, cause lightning and thunder, and influence man. Whether they actually exist or not is unimportant compared to their very great symbology, an understanding of which may be absolutely vital to the survival of the human race. As the Guardians of the Earth Mother, servants of their Cloud Father, they signify all that is beautiful and in harmony in our living world. Their spiritual death in our hearts, that is our inability to be sensitive to our beautiful creation and its preservation, means the material death of our earth by pollution of air and water, destruction of plants and rocks and rivers, and the creeping ugliness of cities until the whole world decays under the terrible blight of man's blindness.

QUETZALCOATL

Quetzalcoatl is the "Lord of the Dawn", sung about in this book, a Great One who brought spiritual awareness and enlightenment to the Indians of America. His name means "the Plumed Serpent", which combines the snake (earth) with the bird (sky) and so the harmony of the two. He appeared in the tenth century as an American Indian, born of a Mixtec mother and Chichimec father, and became the perfect Indian, an American Manifestation. He founded a new religion based on peace and actually changed the face of Ancient America by religious and social reform. He founded the first "Confederation of the Tree", and laid down a prophecy which shatters the imagination of modern man. This book, LORD OF THE DAWN, is about all of that.

4

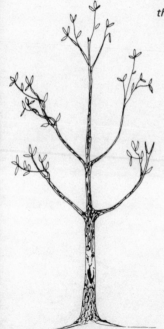

Thirteen Heavens of Decreasing Choice
Nine Hells of Increasing Doom . . . . .
And the "Tree of Life" shall blossom
With a fruit never before Known in
the Creation . . . . .

For
Jessie
and
Good Luck Tomorrow
Your Friend
Tony Shearer

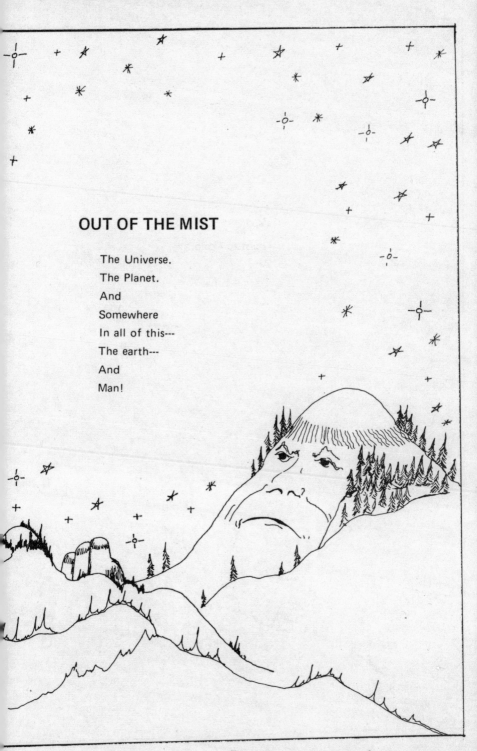

OUT OF THE MIST

The Universe.
The Planet.
And
Somewhere
In all of this---
The earth---
And
Man!

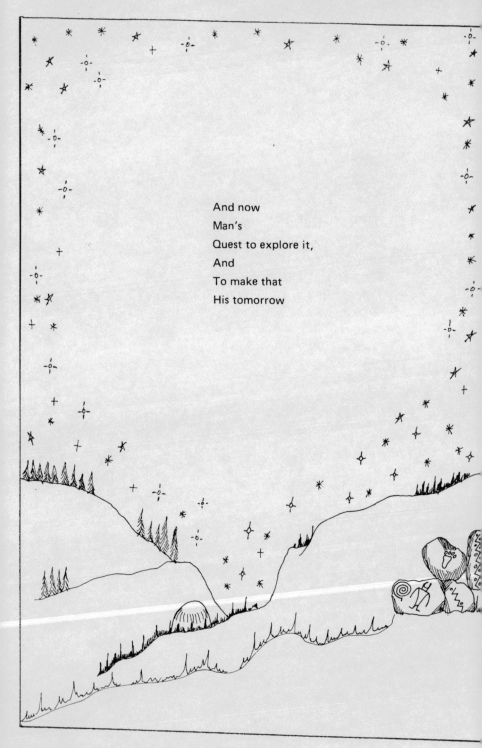

And now
Man's
Quest to explore it,
And
To make that
His tomorrow

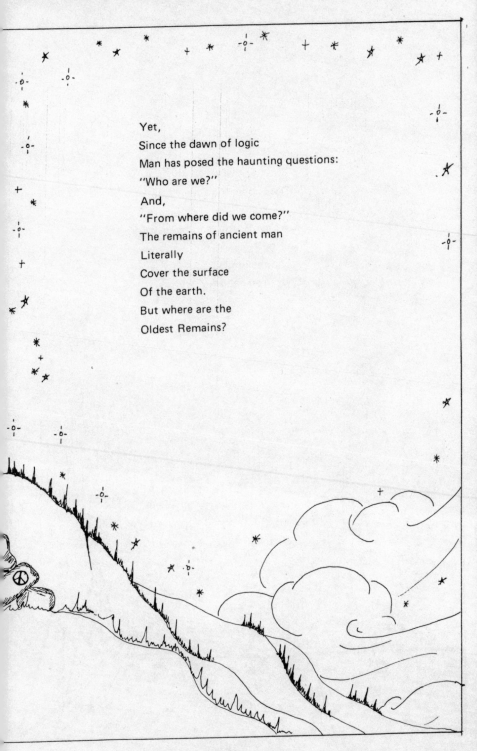

Yet,
Since the dawn of logic
Man has posed the haunting questions:
"Who are we?"
And,
"From where did we come?"
The remains of ancient man
Literally
Cover the surface
Of the earth.
But where are the
Oldest Remains?

And
There
Are those who ask:
"DID we come from the earth,
Or
Did we come from another galaxy?
A world
Beyond the limits
Of our imagination!

Did
We come from the legendary Atlantis?
Or,
Was that story
Only a myth?"
"Did
The same Master Builders
Of the pyramids of Egypt
Also
Build the Pyramid of the Sun
In Mexico?"

"Who was
The white bearded man
Who came to Mexico
And taught
The strange philosophy
Of Peace?"

Was He a Toltec Lord
Or,
Was He
The last survivor
From
A civilization
Which rests on the floor
Of the Pacific?
How
Can we
Learn the answers
To
These questions?

How
Do we
Know what is true
And
What is only imagination?

We ask the people who have made
A life study of man,
Of man's ancient history.
We ask an archeologist.
And
If the archeologist really knows
He points
To the remains
Of ancient man
And
His answer is swift.

Man evolved on this planet.
The oldest remains of man
Are no doubt in Africa.
Atlantis is a myth.

There is no connection
Between
The civilizations of
Mexico
And
Egypt.

The Bearded God of Mexico
Was not a white man.
He was a Mexican.
A Mexican-Indian.
A Toltec.

And. . . .
There are no remains
on the floor of the Pacific.

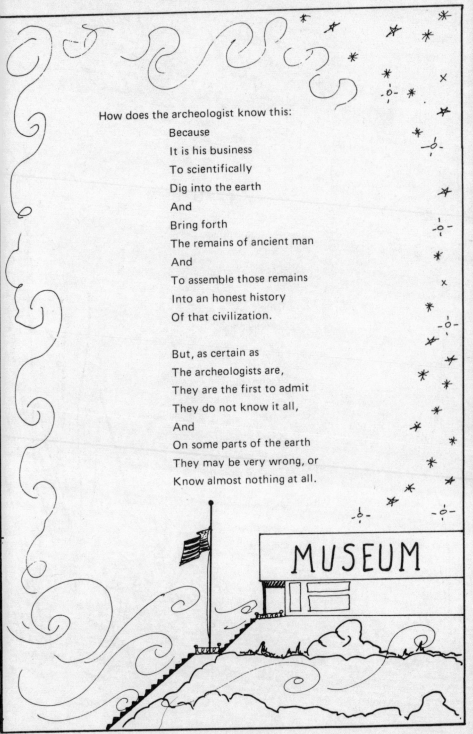

How does the archeologist know this:

    Because
    It is his business
    To scientifically
    Dig into the earth
    And
    Bring forth
    The remains of ancient man
    And
    To assemble those remains
    Into an honest history
    Of that civilization.

    But, as certain as
    The archeologists are,
    They are the first to admit
    They do not know it all,
    And
    On some parts of the earth
    They may be very wrong, or
    Know almost nothing at all.

MUSEUM

LEAVES OF AUTUMN

It's not unlike
Other
Leaves of autumn.

Only a while ago
It was green,
alive,
Now
It is dying.

In time
It will be lost
In the mulch
On a forest floor.

Yet,
In its death
Is beauty.

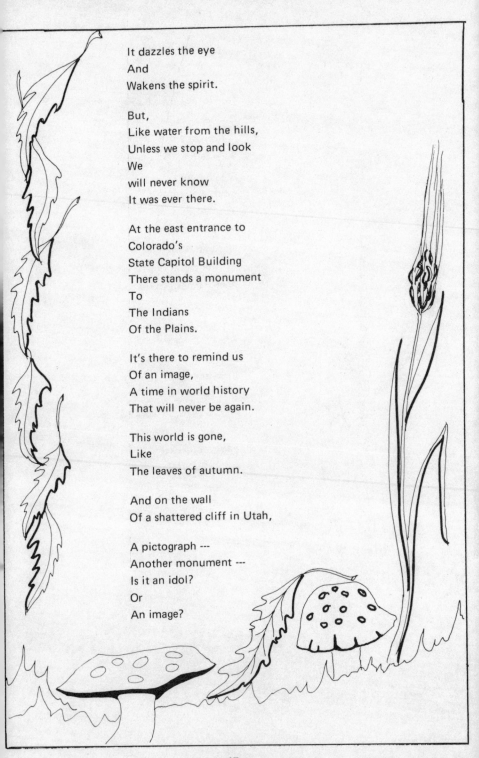

It dazzles the eye
And
Wakens the spirit.

But,
Like water from the hills,
Unless we stop and look
We
will never know
It was ever there.

At the east entrance to
Colorado's
State Capitol Building
There stands a monument
To
The Indians
Of the Plains.

It's there to remind us
Of an image,
A time in world history
That will never be again.

This world is gone,
Like
The leaves of autumn.

And on the wall
Of a shattered cliff in Utah,

A pictograph ---
Another monument ---
Is it an idol?
Or
An image?

In New Mexico
Not far from Santa Fe,
Bandelier National Monument ---
A monument
To a fading race.
Like
Leaves of autumn
Turning to dust.
Mesa Verde
Another monument
To an epic in time
A monument of mud.

Nowhere in the world
Are the poet's words
So true
As in the ruins of Yucatan:

"So fleet these works of man,
Ancient and Holy things
Fade like a dream
Back to earth again."

Incredible to imagine:
      Our altars,
      Our holy things,
      Our cities ---
      Glittering buildings,
      Excited crowds of people,
      Hotels and schools
      Crumbling
      Away into so much rubble.

And what will mankind say of all this
      In a thousand
      Or
      Two thousand years?

Will we be judged then
      By our words
      Or
      By our deeds?

Will we be judged
      By our patriots
      Or
      By our criminals?

I hope in a thousand,
  Or two thousand years,
  Those men can
  Look back at us
  So favorably,
  As our archeologists
  Can
  Look back
  At the noble race
  We
  Took
  This land from. . . .

  The Master Builders of Monte Alban,
  The descendants
  Of the Zapotec,
  Seeds of
  Ancient America.

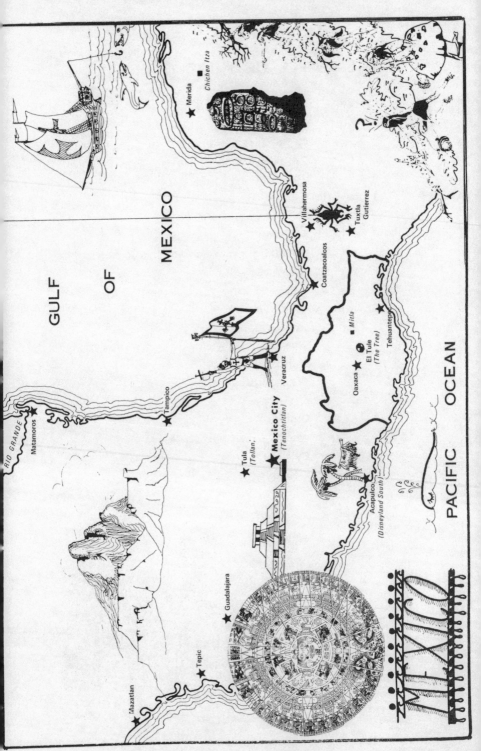

GULF OF MEXICO

PACIFIC OCEAN

RIO GRANDE

Matamoros

Mazatlan

Tepic

Guadalajara

Tula
(Tollan)

Mexico City
(Tenochtitlan)

Tampico

Veracruz

Oaxaca

El Tule
(The Tree)

Mitla

Coatzacoalcos

Villahermosa

Tuxtla
Gutierrez

Tehuantepec

Acapulco
(Disneyland South)

Merida

Chichen Itza

MEXICO

21

THE PEOPLE OF THE CLOUDS

The valley of Oaxaca is
>The homeland
>Of the Zapotecs,
>The People of the Clouds.

The climate in Oaxaca is
>Fair the year around.
>The elevation
>About five thousand two hundred feet
>Above the sea.

In all the world
>I doubt
>There are people
>More gentle
>Than the Zapotecs,
>Nor
>People
>Who have been more abused
>By outside forces.

They have been discriminated against
        In their own land,
        Hated,
        And at times
        Feared..

        Yet,
        Isn't this
        The story
        Of all Indian peoples?

        But,
        The Zapotec emerges
        Victorious
        As Indians will be victorious.

        They
        Insist on
        Being understood.

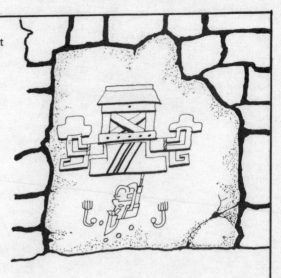

And that understanding begins
        At the summit
        Of their Sacred Mountain,
        In the ancient ruins of Monte Alban
        In the ancient temples
        Of the Zapotec.

        A map
        Shows the excavated
        Area of Monte Alban.
        But
        One must remember
        That the entire city
        Once
        Covered a
        Twenty-five square mile area,

Mostly
On the mountain top,
The ridges,
And
Natural points;

Temples,
Observatories,
Astronomical shrines
And
Sacred Altars,
Pyramids,
Sunken courts,
And stairways.

The tomb area is
To the north,
Beyond the giant stairway.

All of this
is only a fraction
Of the ancient city.

What mysteries lie
Buried
Under those mounds?

What strange people
Transformed
A living stone
Into a temple?

Temples
To
Forgotten Gods.

It is said the ghosts
    Of the ancients
    Still
    Visit these ruins.

    Here
    The old God,
    Quetzalcoatl,
    Still fights human suffering.

    The Rain God
    Still brings the rain
    And
    The Corn God
    Still brings the crops.

    To understand,
    We must know
    Something
    Of the logic
    Of all Mexican Indians,

    Perhaps
    The root
    Logic
    Of all mankind.

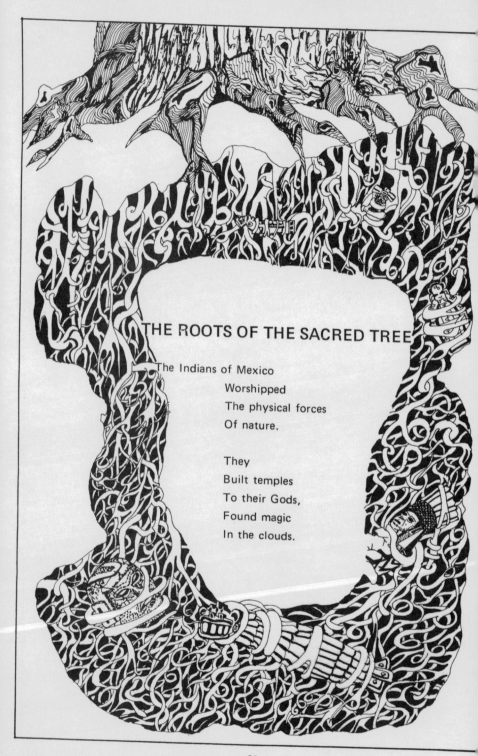

THE ROOTS OF THE SACRED TREE

The Indians of Mexico
         Worshipped
         The physical forces
         Of nature.

         They
         Built temples
         To their Gods,
         Found magic
         In the clouds.

When
There was no water,
When
The rains failed to fall
From the sky,
They
Would call upon
The sky serpent
Call upon their Gods,
the Servants
of the Great Spirit.
For clouds,
For rain.

There was magic in that cool rain,
It turned the corn green
And
Filled the rivers.

They found magic in the lightning
and the thunder ---
The voice
And the hand
Of The Lord of Creation.

They were amazed
By the force
Of the ocean,
Amazed
By its mighty sound!

Good things came from the ocean,
Food,
And
Mystery.

It was good.

Jungles held dark mysteries,
            Secrets.

Wild flowers grew there
            And
            The Indians named them,
            The star flowers,
            Fire flowers
            The lightning flowers
            Flowers of the rains.

The jungle was the home of
            Bright colored parrots
            And
            Chattering monkeys.

            It
            Was the home
            Of night animals,
            Big cats.

The Jaguar was a God
            In disguise!
            He
            Was endowed with
            Supernatural powers.

            The Jaguar
            Had once
            Destroyed
            The earth,
            Devoured mankind.

The jungle was
            Full of wonder,
            And
            Magic.

But, the heavenly bodies,
    The stars,
    were the greatest mysteries.
    The rotation,
    Their disappearing
    And
    Reappearing
    Gave wonder
    To the mind.

The Indians measured
    Time
    And space
    religiously.

    They
    calculated
    An absolutely
    accurate calendar.

    This was only accomplished
    By
    Constant observation
    Of the stars.

    Every day
    The sun
    Must fight
    The stars
    From the sky.

    Every night
    He
    must die.

    The sun
    Was a warrior
    And
    Held great power
    As a God.

Yagul polychrome

Pot sherd from Oaxaca

Mitla polychrome

Fragment of serpent head

Everything in nature
Had
To be balanced
In religion.
The serpent
Was balanced,
So were the
Brightly feathered birds.

Thus
Came the feathered serpent!
He
Was also
The planet Venus
And
The West Wind.

So it was with everything,
A constant fight
Of
Good against evil,
Light against dark.
Until
At last
They had formed
A vast and fantastic civilization.

"Could this be heaven?"
Asked
An early Spaniard
When
First he saw
Tenochtitlan
Now Mexico City.

Unbelievable!
Fantastic!

A
Vast civilization
Of barbaric splendor,
Pagan worship in its
Most magnificent form,
Vision seekers.

Yes, it was these things
And more.
More fantastic than we can imagine
More incredible than you would
Ever dream.

When archeologists first saw Monte Alban,
It was only
High earth mounds,
Very unimpressive.

Some scientists feel
It would have been cheaper
To build a city
Of this size
Than
To excavate one.

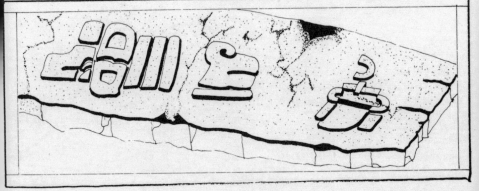

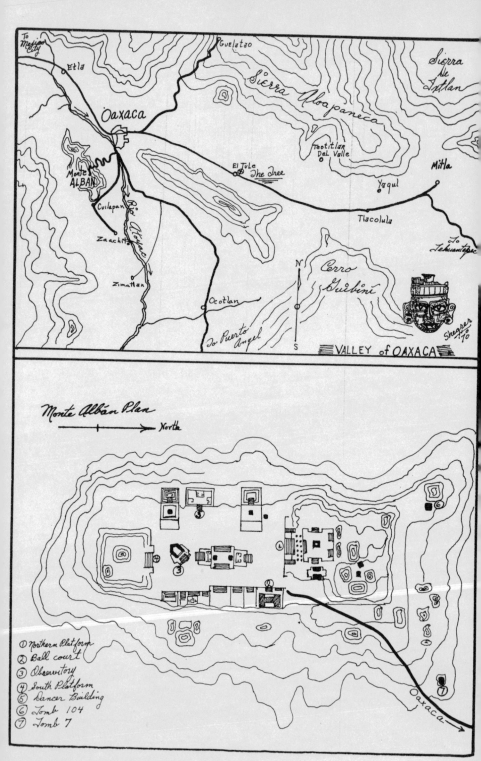

Valley of Oaxaca

Shepper 1.70

Monte Albán Plan

→ North

① Northern Platform
② Ball court
③ Observatory
④ South Platform
⑤ Dancer Building
⑥ Tomb 104
⑦ Tomb 7

MONTE ALBAN - CITY IN THE CLOUDS

Since the dawn of Zapotec history
> This great religious city
> Had
> Gazed down
> On
> The valley of Oaxaca.

Through this valley the Toltecs passed en route to conquer the Mayas of Yucatan.
> The Aztec,
> they came
> and conquered.

Through this valley Quetzalcoatl, the Mexican Messiah passed.

> The Conquistadores,
> They came
> and destroyed.

The long revolutions!

President Juarez was a Zapotec, born in this very valley.
> But time,
> endless time ---
> Monte Alban was lost in time.

Cactus and weeds, dirt and trees,
> had covered the once great city.

In 1931 work commenced to uncover Monte Alban.

Under the direction of the Museum of History and Anthropology part of the city has been restored. Less than one tenth of of Monte Alban has been reconstructed.

We don't really know when the Zapotecs built their first temples on Monte Alban. Scholars say the first people on the Mountain came there about 800 B.C. Others have claimed it to be much older

4½ to 5 feet tall

> dating back to the time of
> Adam and Eve.

The Mixtec (a neighboring tribe) declare that
> the Zapotec have always been
> in the Valley,
> have always
> worshipped on the Sacred Mountain.

The Huecteca, another ancient people of Mexico, tell us that
> the Zapotec are the
> oldest people in the
> entire creation.

They say
> the Zapotec were created
> when Quetzalcoatl
> shaped the valley
> and built the Mountain.

They, say the Huecteca, are
> the first people
> of the First Dawn
> and the Valley of Oaxaca
> is the
> Holy Land of the Americas.

Dancer Stones

The so-called "Dancer Stones"
> are all that can be seen
> of the first,
> the oldest
> works on the Mountain.

But when the Mazatec Indians come to Monte Alban
> to partake of the
> Sacred Mushroom
> they say they can see

Monte Alban I

the invisible remains of
temples and pyramids
far surpassing
those known by modern man.
They say the Dancer Stones
house the spirits
of the ancients
who still come forth
and roam the countryside
on the old Holy Days.
The Zapotecs of the old way laugh at the scientists
who,
with shovel and screen,
try to find
what they believe
is truth.
The old Zapotec says, "The scientists don't know much;
they gather potherbs
and dig into the
Sacred Tombs.
They find only material remains
and
that is not the people.
The people, the Zapotec, are
more spirit than flesh,
and
so it has ever been."
If the scientist knew the spirit,
and really loved the earth,
they would know better
than to dig into
the Holy Places of
their Earth Mother.

The Zapotec points to
the Valley of Oaxaca
and they say

Dancer Stones

Monte Alban I

About 5 feet tall

35

"This is our home-land,
This is our place of sustenance,
This is where we came from,

and

Where we will stay
Till the Creator orders us to leave.
Kill us,
Make us die,
Change us,
Make us like you,
But our spirit
Will not leave this Valley.
We are like the sacred Mountain,
Like the still rocks,
We are like the air,
And the rain,
We are of this place,
And we shall be here,
Where we started,
When the earth is changed
And a new world is born,
We will still be here.
We, the Zapotec,
The Ben'Zaa,
the Cloud People,
Know our place on this earth,
And we migrated from nowhere,
We have always been here,
Oaxaca is our home.

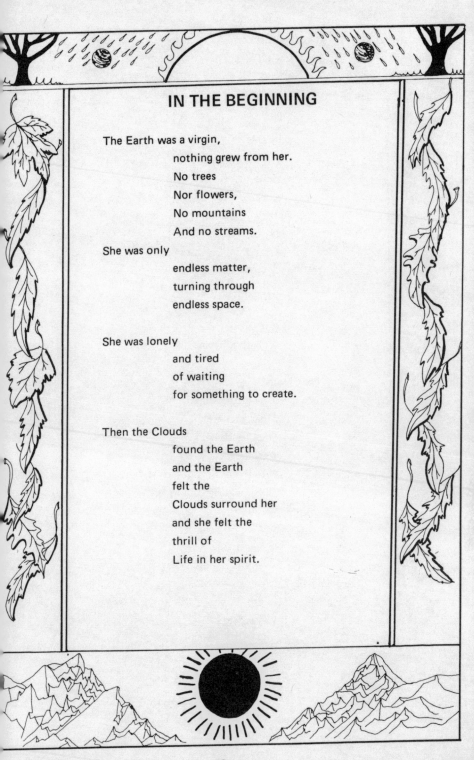

IN THE BEGINNING

The Earth was a virgin,
      nothing grew from her.
      No trees
      Nor flowers,
      No mountains
      And no streams.

She was only
      endless matter,
      turning through
      endless space.

She was lonely
      and tired
      of waiting
      for something to create.

Then the Clouds
      found the Earth
      and the Earth
      felt the
      Clouds surround her
      and she felt the
      thrill of
      Life in her spirit.

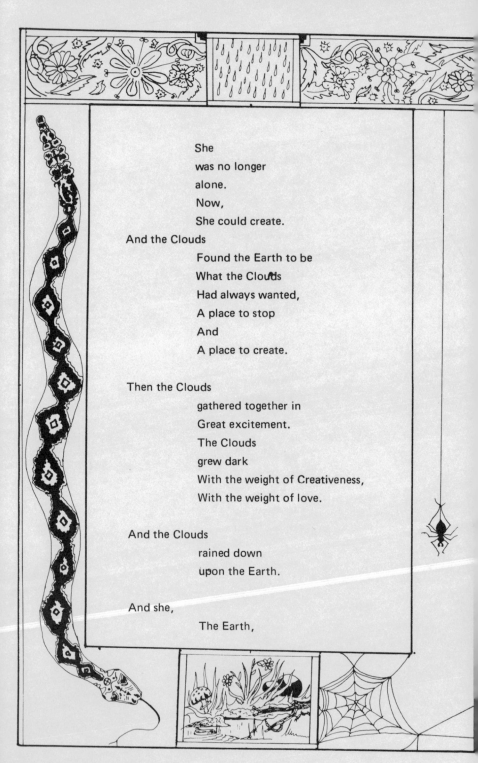

She
was no longer
alone.
Now,
She could create.
And the Clouds
Found the Earth to be
What the Clouds
Had always wanted,
A place to stop
And
A place to create.

Then the Clouds
gathered together in
Great excitement.
The Clouds
grew dark
With the weight of Creativeness,
With the weight of love.

And the Clouds
rained down
upon the Earth.

And she,
The Earth,

Reached up
To touch the Clouds
With mountains of stone
From her breast.

And the

Creative forces of the Clouds
Washed the mountains
And
Formed the rivers.

Then, she,

The Earth
Released the seeds
Of her flesh
And
Trees sprang forth
with leaves.

And grass

Leaped from her flesh
To meet
The fresh rain.
Bushes,
And reeds,
And flowers
Sprang into being,
As a result of
Her love for the rain.

The Clouds

Feeling the force
Of her love,
Rolling thunder
And
Flashing with lightning,
Sacrificed
Part of his own spirit.
And the spirit
Of the rain-drops
Entered into every bush,
And reed,
And flower,
Into every tree
And every living thing.

This was not enough,
Not enough of him,
He lit the sky with lightning
And sent forth his greatest sacrifice,
This came in the form of
Guardians of the Earth.
Tiny spirits,
Pockwatchie spirits,
Tlaloque spirits,
Spirits of the mountains,
Guardians of her breast,
Spirits of the rocks,
Guardians of her love,

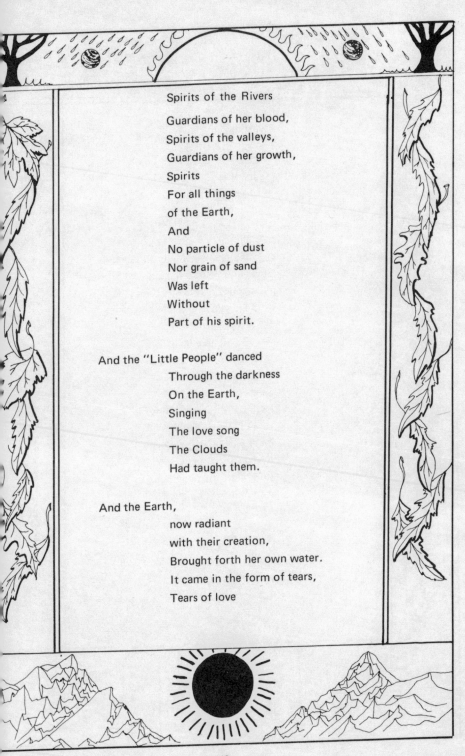

Spirits of the Rivers
Guardians of her blood,
Spirits of the valleys,
Guardians of her growth,
Spirits
For all things
of the Earth,
And
No particle of dust
Nor grain of sand
Was left
Without
Part of his spirit.

And the "Little People" danced
Through the darkness
On the Earth,
Singing
The love song
The Clouds
Had taught them.

And the Earth,
now radiant
with their creation,
Brought forth her own water.
It came in the form of tears,
Tears of love

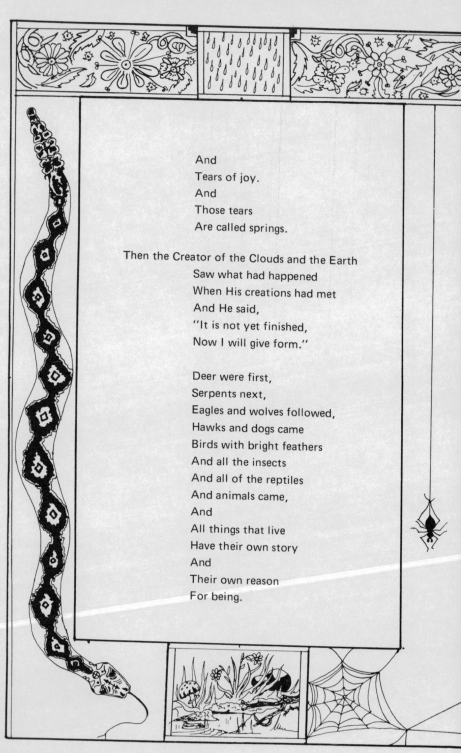

And
Tears of joy.
And
Those tears
Are called springs.

Then the Creator of the Clouds and the Earth
Saw what had happened
When His creations had met
And He said,
"It is not yet finished,
Now I will give form."

Deer were first,
Serpents next,
Eagles and wolves followed,
Hawks and dogs came
Birds with bright feathers
And all the insects
And all of the reptiles
And animals came,
And
All things that live
Have their own story
And
Their own reason
For being.

Then the Creator examined it all
  And said,
  "GOOD.
  Now I will make humans,"
  And immediately
  A man
  Sprang from the oldest Tree on Earth,
And in that same instant
  A woman sprang from the same Tree.
  And that Tree is the "Tree of Life."
When they reached
  The dirt,
  And stood up,
  They started
  To look for
  Each other in the darkness.
When they found each other
  They started to look for food.
They looked for a long time,
  Walked many miles in the darkness,
  Crossed many rivers
  And
  Drank the tears
  Of many Springs.

When at last

        they found themselves

        back at the "Tree of Life"

        They said,

        "Tree, we are hungry,

        Where is food?"

And the "Tree of Life" said,

        "Take a leaf from me,

        And

        Put it in your Earth Mother

        And

        You shall have the perfect food."

The man and the woman took a leaf

        From the ancient Tree

        And

        Put it in the flesh of their

        Earth Mother

        And

        A stalk of corn appeared.

And at that same moment

        The woman had two babies (twins)

And at that same moment

        The sun was born.

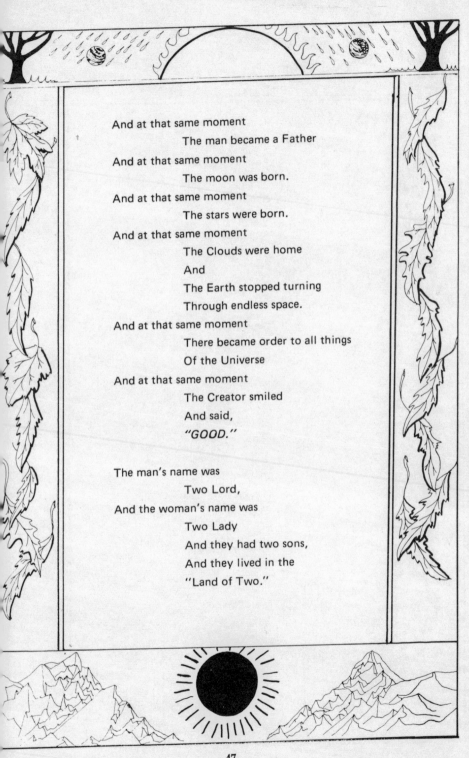

And at that same moment
　　　　The man became a Father
And at that same moment
　　　　The moon was born.
And at that same moment
　　　　The stars were born.
And at that same moment
　　　　The Clouds were home
　　　　And
　　　　The Earth stopped turning
　　　　Through endless space.
And at that same moment
　　　　There became order to all things
　　　　Of the Universe
And at that same moment
　　　　The Creator smiled
　　　　And said,
　　　　"GOOD."

The man's name was
　　　　Two Lord,
And the woman's name was
　　　　Two Lady
　　　　And they had two sons,
　　　　And they lived in the
　　　　"Land of Two."

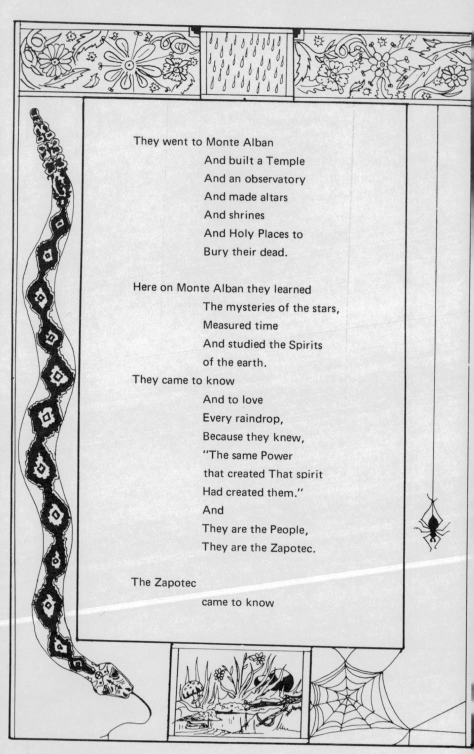

They went to Monte Alban
    And built a Temple
    And an observatory
    And made altars
    And shrines
    And Holy Places to
    Bury their dead.

Here on Monte Alban they learned
    The mysteries of the stars,
    Measured time
    And studied the Spirits
    of the earth.
They came to know
    And to love
    Every raindrop,
    Because they knew,
    "The same Power
    that created That spirit
    Had created them."
    And
    They are the People,
    They are the Zapotec.

The Zapotec

    came to know

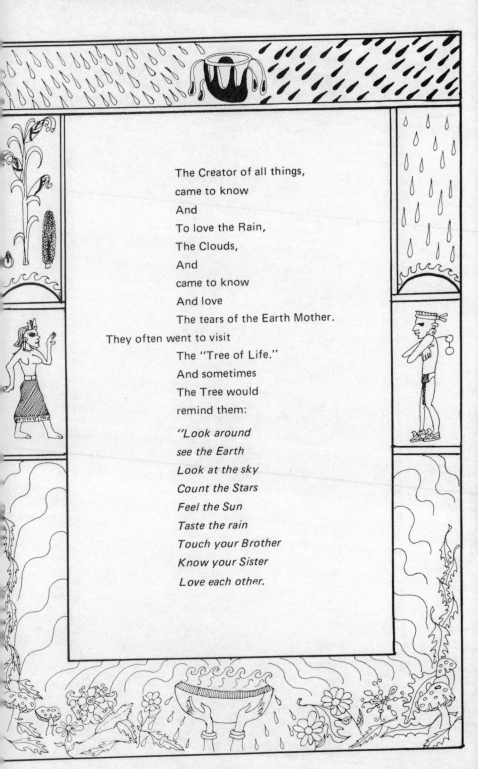

The Creator of all things,
came to know
And
To love the Rain,
The Clouds,
And
came to know
And love
The tears of the Earth Mother.
They often went to visit
The "Tree of Life."
And sometimes
The Tree would
remind them:

*"Look around
see the Earth
Look at the sky
Count the Stars
Feel the Sun
Taste the rain
Touch your Brother
Know your Sister
Love each other.*

49

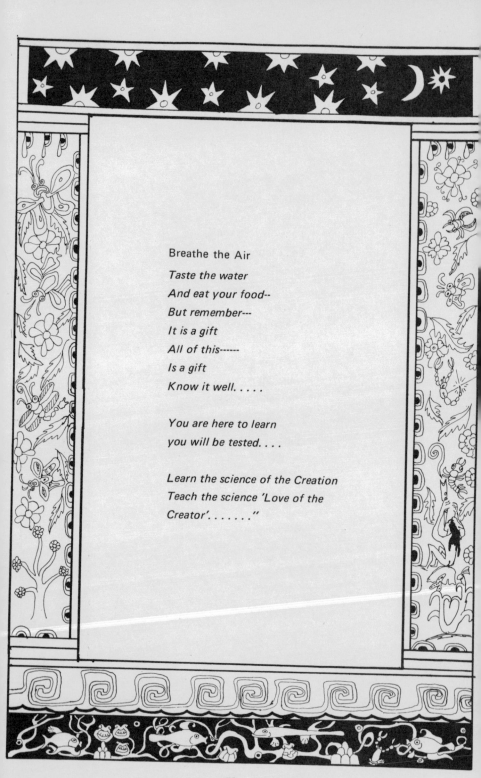

Breathe the Air

Taste the water

And eat your food--

But remember---

It is a gift

All of this------

Is a gift

Know it well. . . . .

You are here to learn

you will be tested. . . .

Learn the science of the Creation

Teach the science 'Love of the

Creator'. . . . . . ."

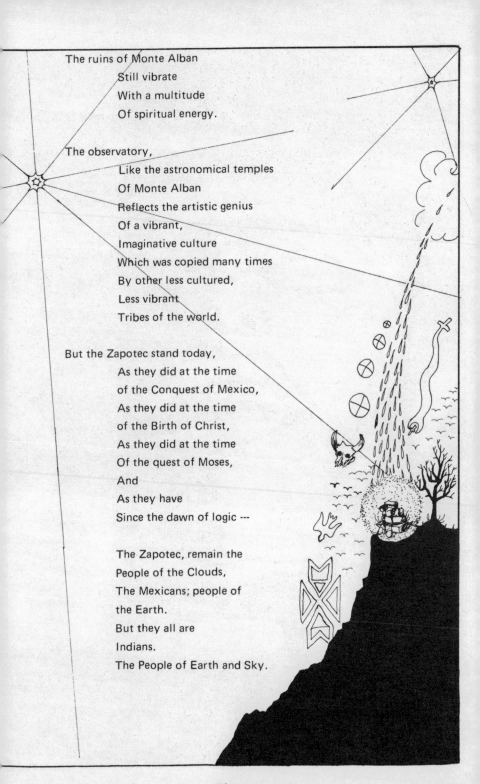

The ruins of Monte Alban
    Still vibrate
    With a multitude
    Of spiritual energy.

The observatory,
    Like the astronomical temples
    Of Monte Alban
    Reflects the artistic genius
    Of a vibrant,
    Imaginative culture
    Which was copied many times
    By other less cultured,
    Less vibrant
    Tribes of the world.

But the Zapotec stand today,
    As they did at the time
    of the Conquest of Mexico,
    As they did at the time
    of the Birth of Christ,
    As they did at the time
    Of the quest of Moses,
    And
    As they have
    Since the dawn of logic ---

    The Zapotec, remain the
    People of the Clouds,
    The Mexicans; people of
    the Earth.
    But they all are
    Indians.
    The People of Earth and Sky.

THE FUNERAL

Remember, these people built their religious center
    On the top of a mountain.
    There has never been
    An implement
    Of war or torture
    Found
    On this mountain.

Everything had to be carried
    To the lofty summit of Monte Alban.
    Food and water,
    Stone and clay,
    Fuel
    For the eternal fire
    That
    Was kept burning
    By twelve virgins.

And all the kings,
    The scientists,
    The priests and artists,
    The great people,
    were all buried
    On the mountain.
    Offerings were made to the dead.
    The dead were buried in tombs.
    The tombs were
    often
    Shaped like a cross.

Special note should be made here
    regarding the Zapotec
    And
    Their apparent
    Involvement

With
The World
Of the Dead and
The Unborn.

The following is a poetic description
of my own personal
interpretation
of an ancient funeral.

The description comes partly from
Ancient drawings,
And
Partly from
Present day reflections
Of ancient traditions.

I once witnessed a funeral
In the
Village of Mixtequilla,
Oaxaca.
It so impressed me
At the time
That I later
Incorporated the idea
Into my slide show.
Needless to say
The sequence is highly
speculative,
But,
I feel it is
Worthy of consideration
In lieu
Of the fact
That no other description
Has, as yet,
been submitted.

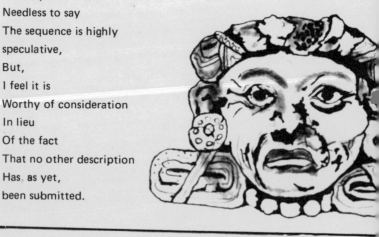

The body of the dead was
       Wrapped in a cotton blanket,
       Followed by a long procession
       He was
       Carried across the great plaza,
       The People
       Sang a sad song.

In the dark of night
       He was carried
       To the magician's pyramid
       To the sorcerer's temple.
The magician would
       Try to
       Restore life
       To the body.
In a clear crystal chalice
       He would concoct
       A formula,
       Pass it over sacred incense,
       Flavor it with herbs
       And magic color potions.
The liquid of the formula was
       Then poured
       Into the lips of the dead.
The magician waited,
       Said magic words,
       Made magic signs.
       He attempted
       To put the magic formula
       Into motion.
       But,
       At last
       He failed.

The friends and the family wept,
       Mourned
       For the dead man.

The torches were lit
From the sacred fire
By twelve virgins
And the procession
Continued
Across the plaza
To the foot
Of the
Giant stairway.

The High Priest was called upon.
Permission to
Bring the body
Up
Was asked.

It was granted by the High Priest,
And the body
was
Slowly carried
Up
To
The last altar.

Here the priest dressed the dead
In his finest clothes,
Blessed him,
Said nice things
About him.
The Priest
Assured the family
It
Would be
Cared for.
The family
Presented
The High Priest
With the

Dead man's
Funeral Urn,
The patron of
The dead man.
Each
Person of importance
Had one.

A farewell speech was made by the High Priest
Kind words
With deep meaning.

"He is gone from amongst us.
We will
Miss the sound of his voice
His face,
We will miss his eyes.
His ears
Will no longer hear the thunder,
The rain
Will no longer fall upon his lips
His feet
Will no longer leave tracks
In the dirt,
But
He now knows
What we desire to know;
He
Has gone
Beyond the thunder."

Gifts and offerings were then made
To the dead.
Corn and beans,
Flowers and jewels,
Gold and jade,
Strings of beads,
Turquoise,

Onyx and silver,
Not to be taken to the next world,
But
Because these things are beautiful.

The body was then taken to the tomb.
He was put inside.
The offerings
Were put with him.
The funeral urn
Was set in place,
And
The tomb was closed,
Sealed
And blessed.

This was the funeral
of even
The greatest king.

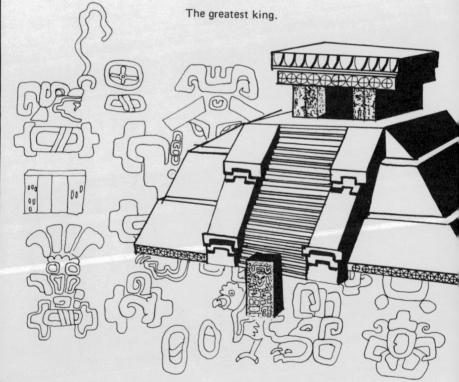

THE MAGIC JAGUAR BONES

One of the most fascinating traits
>> Of the Zapotecs
>> Was
>> Their tomb complex.

Recent excavations of the Oaxaca area
>> Reveal
>> That the
>> People of the Clouds
>> Have been using
>> Tombs
>> For many thousands of years.

The most famous tomb in Oaxaca
>> And the richest tomb
>> Of the Americas
>> Is known simply
>> As
>> Tomb 7, Monte Alban,
>> Opened by
>> Dr. Alfonso Caso
>> In 1931.

The debris that buried the court
>> Was cleared away
>> And
>> Pits were dug
>> To find the roof,
>> The stone slab
>> Was removed

From
The vaulted ceiling
And the tomb
Was opened.

Now,
Dr. Caso lowered himself
Into the tomb,
With a flashlight
In his hand.
As his eyes slowly
Became
Accustomed to the darkness
He realized
He
Was in a most unusual tomb.

The paintings on the wall
Told a religious story,
The funeral urn above the door,
Was of extreme importance.
It was
The God of Wind and Air.

But the extreme wealth of the tomb
Was immediately apparent.
Jewels of extraordinary value,
Masks of solid gold,
And beads of gold,
Golden bracelets,
And fan handles of gold
Golden rings
And buckles of solid gold.
One necklace
Of pearls the size of marbles,
Mosaics of turquoise,
Ornaments of crystal and alabaster,
Necklaces of silver and obsidian,

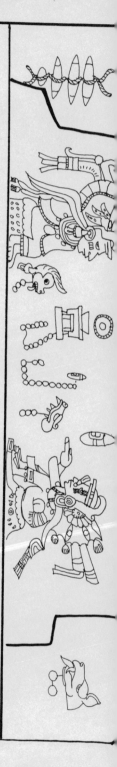

Jade, jet and amber carved
Into religious designs,
Carved stone blocks,
And
The finest of Mixtec pottery.

The tomb held over 500 individual offerings
Plus
Hundreds of tiny golden bells
Thousands of golden beads.

But the glittering treasures of Tomb 7 were dwarfed by a
collection of 34 Jaguar bones,
Carefully carved,
And
Delicately inlaid
With
Jade and turquoise,
The bones
Were covered
With
Hieroglyphic writings.

The physical remains
Found in the tomb
Were
Of eight men
And
One woman.

They seemed to have belonged to
a religious clan,
The leader
And
Most important person
Was
A frightful syphilitic giant,
A true human monster
Over nine feet tall.

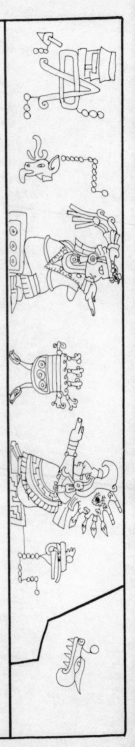

It was later determined that
　　　　He had died of a brain tumor.

The discovery of Tomb 7 amazed the world, and for ten years or more the contents of the tomb were examined by every authority of renown in the world, the treasure traveling around the world, viewed with value by all who held it.
　At last
　　　　It returned to
　　　　The Valley of Oaxaca!
　　　　There
　　　　One
　　　　May visit it today.

Alfonso Caso has devoted
　　　　Most of his life
　　　　To the ruins of Monte Alban
　　　　And
　　　　To the history
　　　　Of the people
　　　　Who prove to be
　　　　The inheritors
　　　　Of those proud temples,
　　　　Now in ruin.

Dr. Caso readily admits
　　　　The greatest treasure
　　　　Of Tomb 7
　　　　was not
　　　　the wealth of gold and jade,
　　　　But was, instead
　　　　The collection of Jaguar bones,
　　　　so delicately designed.
　　　　When assembled correctly
　　　　The bones tell a story.
　　　　And the story proves to be
　　　　The most mysterious history
　　　　Of ancient America.

It is,
In fact,
The story of Quetzalcoatl
As the Mixtec knew it
In the Thirteenth Century
Of our era.

Autumn

Comes to the high country
And
Marks the end
Of the cycle of life,
And all that had been bright in Spring
And green in summer
Turns gold in autumn
And prepares for
A new cycle of life,

What is true in nature

Seems true of the Zapotec.

The People of the Clouds

Lived in the valley
And
Worshipped on the Mountain,
On Monte Alban.

There

They had built their temples,
and tombed their dead.

There

They had worshipped the forces of nature,
Measured time
and calculated a perfect calendar.

There

They had learned the mysteries
Of
The Tree of Life.

But autumn had come for the Zapotec,
And
In autumn
Everything dies a little.
Zapotec art shows a decay of civilization,
But
The decay
Was not to last.
Forces in the North
Had already been set into motion,
By the middle of the
Ninth Century A.D.
The Zapotec could
Feel the forces
And
Realize the change
Which was transforming
Not only Oaxaca
But
All of Mexico,
And
Perhaps
Most of North America.

Tlaloques (Aztec-Toltec name for the little people) on temple wall, Valley of Mexico. Songs are shown issuing from their mouths.
Painting by Tony Shearer, using photograph of actual carvings.

Pockwatchies (little people of the woods) on Bald Mountain
Color painting by Tony Shearer - Autumn of 1967

Mitla Temple

Grecas of Mitla

Faces for a Tomb in Valley of Oaxaca

Great Tree at El Tule

Ancient symbolic figure of Quetzalcoatl - painting by Tony Shearer

Ancient symbolic figure of Tezcatlipoca - painting by Charlotte Espinoza

Palenque Stone

This ink drawing is a copy of the 7 x 12½ foot monolithic stone found in the tomb beneath the Temple of Inscriptions at Palenque, in the state of Chiapas, Mexico. The stone carving was not painted and the selection of colors here is purely by taste and has nothing whatever to do with the symbolism of the Mayan Indians who did the original work.

The stone is actually a lid for a coffin which was carved from the living stone under the Temple. This tomb could be reached only by a stairway which entered the temple at the top and then led some 65 feet down into the interior of the Temple.

When this stone lid was moved away it was found that another lid had been placed under the first lid in a very peculiar fashion, fitting perfectly into a cavity carved to hold it with absolute precision and provided with thirteen moveable stone stoppers. When this highly polished second stone was removed, the skeleton of a man came to view. The man is believed to have been "about" 45 years old, very tall and literally covered with jade ornaments. The inside of the coffin was painted with dark red cinnabar. The man had been buried in a red robe, which had perished, but the remains clung to the bones and the jade jewels.

It is agreed that the Temple of Inscriptions is a true temple-pyramid, resembling the Egyptian pyramids in many ways, and that it is unlike other temples found in the Americas. A great degree of attainment must have been realized by the builders of this fantastic temple. And one wonders if such a fascinating tomb, found in such an unusual city as Palenque, does not suggest greater importance than is now realized from mere physical remains. Even themselves, these remains point to Palenque as the scene of a most unusual happening.

It was this stone and the Temple of Inscriptions that first made me aware of the prophecy of the Thirteen Heavens and the Nine Hells. It is my belief that the young man on the face of the stone is none other than Tezcatlipoca, offering his right foot as a sacrifice to the Earth Monster, that the Tree of Life might survive, and that one day the Twins would come forth from the mouth of the Plumed Serpent (symbol of Creation), and save the world or create a new one.

Palenque Stone - from Temple of the Inscription
Color painting by Tony Shearer

Tree and the Church

An ancient church now stands in the shadow of the *"Tree"* recalling its sacredness.

Tree with Children

Part of the trunk of the *"Zapotec Tree of Life,"* El Tule, Oaxaca in Mexico.

"LORD OF THE DAWN"

The Lord of the Dawn is coming

Covered with precious feathers,

He is coming

Carrying a serpent staff,

He is coming.

The "Giver of Life" is coming.

The "Creator of All" is coming.

The "Lord of the Dawn" is coming.

The old magician,
>   the sorcerer of Monte Alban
>   Studied
>   The Charts of Time,
>   Read
>   The old prophecies.
Then
>   He stood up
>   And
>   Untied his robe,
>   Letting it fall in a heap
>   At his feet.
>   He turned to the altar
>   Of Cosijo (the rain god)
>   And
>   With many gestures
>   Of his hands
>   And
>   His body
>   He prayed
>   In this way:

"Two heavens of time have we waited.
Now
The cycle of the second heaven is near its close.
Now
The time has come for your return.

"Let it be true:
Let it not be the imagining of foolish people,
Of wistful people.
Let it be true.

"Two heavens of time have we waited.
Let it be now."

The prophecies of the Manifestation were well-known to the people of Ancient Mexico.

And when the time grew near
  The people
  Felt the fulfillment
  More in their hearts
  Than
  In their logic.

The news of the nearness of the
  "Promised Day"
  Spread throughout the land.
  From seashore to seashore
  The word
  Was carried.
  "He is coming."

In the Maya Land,
  From Guatemala
  To Yucatan
  The people listened,
  And listened,
  And looked around.
  They studied
  What
  They could see.
  And what they saw
  Was bad.
The Maya, who had hosted the Lord of the Dawn
  In the beginning,
  Had,
  Since his departure,
  Turned away from him
  And
  Taken up the earthly pleasures
  Of
  The Jaguar Cult.

Now,

>The people studied
>What they had done.
>"We have been wrong!"
>They said at last,
>*"We*
>*didn't believe*
>*It could be.*

But now

>*We feel it in our hearts,*
>*See the changes in our children.*

Now

>*We must right the wrong."*

The Jaguar Clans were murdered,

>Their temples burned,
>Their idols smashed.

The entire Mayan civilization crumbled

>Into pathetic ruins.
>And the people
>Rushed
>From the burning cities
>To the forest
>And attempted
>To build new temples
>To
>The Lord of the Dawn.
>Build a temple in His honor,
>Build a temple to the Morning Star,
>Build a shrine to the Tree of Life,
>*"Hurry*
>*He is coming. . . ."*

The Valley of Oaxaca was no exception.

>The magical powers
>Of the Jaguar Cult
>Had long held the people in thrall,
>But
>With the word of His coming

The Zapotec rose up
In religious rebellion
And
Crushed the source
That
Had enslaved their minds.

So it was throughout the land.
Indication of this prophecy's
fulfillment
Has been found
In such distant places as
Saint Louis, Missouri,
The Ohio River mounds,
In the Rio Grande Valley
And as far South as
Columbia
And Peru,
An area roughly,
nine times as large as the
Holy Land
And as large
As the civilized part of
Ancient China.

The ruins of Tikal
In Guatemala, that
Had
An estimated population of 100,000
people,
was abandoned
And
Was left in ruins
At this time.
Tikal
was the home
of the greatest
of the Jaguar Clans.

Monte Alban, some twenty-five square miles
of religious barracks,
temples,
Pyramids
And
Astronomical structures,
Was abandoned
By the Zapotec.

(Later,
It thrived again
Under Mixtec lords.)

City after city
Was abandoned
And
Left in ruin,
Old religious cults
Were destroyed.

But high in the Sierras,
South of present day Mexico City,
Stood the old temples of Quetzalcoatl
At a place called Xochicalco.

There

The order of Quetzalcoatl,
Had retreated
After the fall of Teotihucan
One hundred and four years before.
And the old Priests
Of Quetzalcoatl
Held
The prophecy in order.

They knew
What no one else knew.

For
They had been chosen
As the Guardians of His sacred Tablets.
They knew
When he would be born,
They knew
He would be born there,
At Xochicalco.

They waited
And waited,
But
The day had not yet come
And
They knew it.

"Thirteen Heavens of Decreasing Choice, Nine
Hells of Increasing Doom----

Thirteen, 52-year cycles of Choice; Nine, 52-year
cycles of Doom

"And the "Tree of Life" shall blossom
With a fruit never before known in the creation.
And that fruit shall be the New Spirit of Men."

Where had this come from?
        The Priests of Xochicalco knew.
        They knew it had come from the source.
        They knew it came
        From the City of the Serpent,
        From the jungle low-lands,
        long ago,
        When He appeared on Earth.
        They knew
        He had left this prophecy behind
        and
        Told them

He would return to remind them
And
To enlighten them.

"You will not know me by my miracles," He had said.
"Magicians can perform miracles.
You will know me by the 'Tree',
But
We *will* do miracles," He said.

His signs were many,
The Morning Star,
The Sacred Twin,
The Tree of Life,
The Feathered Serpent,
But now,

The Lord of the Dawn is coming!

THE MOTHER OF THE DAWN

"Come quickly",
>
> Cried the children.
> "We found her in the bushes,
> She is alone
> And
> She is hurt,
> Covered with mud,
> And
> Scratched by thorn bushes
> She has walked far
> And
> She has come to see
> Her uncle Salavi,
> She is hurt,
> She is pretty."

Chimalma had arrived,
>
> Niece of Old Salavi,
> The elder of Xochicalco.

She was taken to a bed
>
> And made comfortable
> Washed
> And fed
> And covered with a
> Soft cotton blanket
> And
> She slept
> For a day
> And a night.

When she woke
>
> Salavi was beside her
> And she wept.

Salavi comforted her
And asked
Of her father, his brother,
Dead,
She said.

He asked of her mother, his friend,
Her answer
Was the same.
Dead.

Then she told him what had happened.
Told him of her love,
Told him of the barbarians
And he said
He knew that, and that now
He knew her part in this long story.

He asked
If she would come to the temple,
And tell the Council of Quetzalcoatl
Her story.
She said that
She would do that.

So Salavi went to the "Shrine of the Dawn"
and prayed
Until he was told that she was
At the temple of
The Council of Quetzalcoatl
Then
He went there to hear her,
And
To help.

"I was washing my hair in a waterfall
And he came then
And watched me.

At first
I was afraid,
But
He was not as bad as he looked.
He was a warrior
Of the Chichimeca:
He was their leader.
His name,
Mixcoatl, (Cloud Serpent),
He followed me home
And
Talked to my father.

Mixcoatl wanted me,
Wanted me to be his wife,
He wanted me to
Make children for him.
He said he would make a good world
For everyone,
So our children could live in beauty.

No, said my father,
My father told him that I was
Chimalma
A virgin of the Temple of the Dawn,
I could not marry.

Mixcoatl was not young,
He was an older man,
His love for me
Was strong and pure,
I could realize
What he was.

At last my father said,
'Yes.'
And I
Became Mixcoatl's wife.
He was a warrior,
But he was good.
I could see his spirit

And
It was white
As the shadow of the Creator,
He was good,
My heart and my spirit
Belonged to him,
I was happy.

We left my village and
went to
The Chichimeca camp,
In the north.

We could not have each other
Till the marriage
Had been consecrated by
His brothers.

His brothers refused.
They said
They would conquer all of Mexico
And
Girls like me
Would become their slaves.
They said
We would clean their filth
And
Eat their trash
And
At night
We would sleep at their feet.

Mixcoatl became outraged.
I told him
' No!'
But
He drew his war axe
And fought

It was a terrible fight.

    Mixcoatl fought like
    A wild animal,
    Like a Jaguar.
    His axe swung in all directions,
    and men fell before him
    Like leaves in a whirlwind.

    Then
    An arrow struck him
    In his chest,
    And yet more arrows came,
    And Mixcoatl fell
    Into the shadows.

    His last words sounded
    like a prayer---
    'Run!'
    He said.
    And I rushed off
    Into the darkness.

The last I saw of my husband
    was
    The two fingers of his left hand
    Separated in the shape of a "V".

    I ran
    And hid.
    The Chichimecas
    Were always near.
    Somehow,
    By some strange source
    I was not caught.
    On I traveled,
    Sleeping
    In the branches of trees
    In the daytime

And
Traveling at night.

Each village I would reach
Had already been visited
By the Chichimecas,
Already destroyed
And
The sign of their God
Was left behind.
Tezcatlipoca
Had been there.
Tezcatlipoca,
The dark lord
Of human sacrifice.

When I reached my home,
My father's village,
I found the whole town
Destroyed
And
Everyone dead
And
Branded with the sign of
Tezcatlipoca.
Their hearts were gone,
And
The right foot
Of each Holy Man
Had been stolen.

I left there and
Thought to come here.
But instead
I became lost
And
Found myself at Chapultepec
(Hill of the Grasshopper)

I tried to go
To the lake for water
But I
Fell into the mud.
I
Became stuck there.
I turned
And tried to move
But I was fast.

It was dark.

A strange thing happened.
People were coming toward me,
I thought they were Chichimecas
Come to kill me,
But
They were not.
They were
People from the future.
They carried a great cactus
And
A serpent
And
They were weeping
Because they had lost
Their eagle.
They came to me
And talked.
They told me
They were servants
Of the
"Lord of the Dawn"
And that
They loved me,
They had to help me.

An old lady with white hair
Came forward then

And
Wiped my face
And called me
Earth Mother
And
Dawn Child,
She said
I was covered with beauty.

Then all of the stars
Turned green in the sky,
Green as jade.
And
One very bright star
Fell from the sky,
Stopped above my stomach,
Glowed very bright.
Then
Entered my stomach
Through my womb,
And
I fell to sleep.

I had no dream,
Not really,
Only a feeling of
Great contentment
And joy.

When I awoke the old white haired woman
Was still there near me,
She spoke,
' Mixcoatl is waiting for you
Beyond the Morning Star,
He is waiting,
Hurry and have the baby,
He is waiting for you. '

She stood up and
Walked away.
She said no more.

Now
I am here
At Xochicalco
with all of you
And my dear uncle Salavi.
I have no husband,
But I know
I will soon have a baby."

"Yes,"
Said Salavi,
"The child will be born
            In the ninth moon,
            Always in the ninth moon
On the day of One Reed,
In the year of One Reed---
In the ninth moon."

And the old priests of Xochicalco
All sighed together,

"Grandfather
 Grandfather
 Grandfather
 Grandfather."

They wept,
They knew it was true,
"The Lord of the Dawn"
Was coming.

THE VISION OF SALAVI

Salavi left the Temple of Quetzalcoatl
        And went into the barracks
        of the Nonoalca
        And chose twenty of them
        To go forth into all parts
        Of the land,
        To the extent of all directions
        And to tell
        Everyone they encountered
        That
        He would soon be on Earth.

He reminded them that
        No one will believe you.
        "That
        Is exactly as it is meant to be."
        Salavi laughed.
        "But
        Tell them anyway,
        Tell them once more,
        Then
        Tell them they have been told---
        And
        Leave---"

Salavi then returned to
        The Temple of the Dawn
        And prepared for
        A vision.

        Four days he fasted in the Temple,
        No food
        No water
        No words from his lips
        No sleep.

Then
He rested
Slept for a full night
Arose in the morning before the sunlight
Ate raw fruit
Drank of the cactus tea
Drank of Water.

He cried for the vision.
His song was heard throughout the city.
And all who heard
Knew why.
No one understood the words
To the Ancient Chant.
Those words, and
That song
Were said to
Have come from another world.
A world now buried beneath
The rolling tides of salt water
In the
Great Eastern Sea,
And now known only by
The elders of the
Council of Quetzalcoatl.

"Evoke the nether world,
Evoke the spirit of the Earth Mother,
The voice of the Clouds,
Evoke the Heart of Heaven
And
The Heart of the Earth,
And quest for the hidden words."

Salavi's vision came from
An ancient tree.
A tree
He had never seen

But
Had often heard about.

The vision came
Through the branches
Of the tree
And
He wondered
If this could be
The "Tree of Life."

The answer came back
"Yes."

He questioned
Of Mixcoatl
And the Chichimeca.
The answer
Came from the roots of the Great Tree,
Came to him
In this way.

"The Chichimeca are as much a part of this story
As is
The Feathered Serpent.
Without them
The Manifestation
Would not be true,
Would not be complete.

The Chichimeca are
From a faraway land
On the other side of your Earth-land,
On the other side of your Earth-mother,
And they,
Like you
Are very important
To the Creation of All Things.

Chichimeca
means
People of Dog Lineage,
Descendant of a man called Dog.
This man
Was a most important
servant of the Creation
In another time,
And they,
The Chichimeca
Are his descendants.

Mixcoatl was
Their Gifted One,
The last
Of their seed.
He
Is the Burning Bush
Of This Land.

Mixcoatl,
Cloud Serpent,
Milky Way,
The
Tree of the Sky,
You can be sure that
He was faithful
To his very death."

The vision became bright now, and continued.

"Tezcatlepoca is not a Chichimeca idea,
He belongs to your people.
If
He is blood thirsty
That is because
The people want blood,
He is a God
An idol

A creation of man.
He comes
From
Your choice of
The first two heavens.

Know him well,
Learn his habits,
Learn his power,
Because
Man
Has created him
And
He
Will be here
Until
The end of the Ninth Hell.
Then
He will remove his mask
And
You will be surprised
Who
He really is."

The vision had passed.

The Little People,
           The Pockwatchies
           And the Tlaloques
           Danced
           From hill to hill,
           Down
           Every moon-bathed path they went,
           Singing a new song,
           One never heard before,
           Not even by them.
           On and on they went

Through woods
And over desert,
Singing as they danced.

The Pockwatchies,
The Little People
Were thrilled with the news of
Fulfillment.
They carried the news
From hill to hill
From wood to wood.

In their tiny hearts they knew what was coming.
These
Little guardians of the Earth
Knew
That one day
They
Would have to face
The brunt of man's ignorance,
Yet
They danced on
Regardless,
Laughing
And singing
Of the wonders of the Creator,
For they knew that

All things that must be
Must be in balance
And
That takes practice.

THE DAWN CHILD PROPHECY

"It's a boy!"
Cried the children.
"It's a boy!"
The word was carried
By the children
From
House to House
Of Xochicalco.

The child
was greeted
With
Great excitement.
He is born,
They said.

The excitement
Turned
To wonderment,
And a
Sort of despair
When
The news came forth. . . .
Chimalma,
She who walked in beauty,
Has passed
Into
The world of the dead,
Has returned
To her Earth Mother,
Her
Spirit
Has gone.

She
Has borne

The Sacred One,
Now
She
Has passed through
The gates
Of
The other world.

She is now
With Mixcoatl
In
The land of green light,
Beyond
The Morning Star.
Chimalma
Had
Given birth
To the long-awaited
Dawn Child,
And
As the prophecy
Had predicted
She died.
Her funeral was simple.
A grave
Within the temple walls.
On the grave
Was placed a
Dead bough
Of an old tree.

The baby boy arrived on Earth
On the
Day One Reed,
In the
Year One Reed,
Exactly as
The prophecy said.

The Sacred Tablets told
Of His birthday
And
Laid out a
Tentative description
Of His life.

Those Tablets
Went further
To describe
That this
Entire epic,
Which
Was now
Taking place
Was but
a fragment
Of what was yet
To come.

The Sacred Tablets,
So faithfully guarded
By the
Council of Quetzalcoatl
Predicted the future
Of
The entire continent.
It was not a
Vague prophecy,
But rather
One of
Eminent magnitude.

Using the Fifty-two year cycle
Of the
Sacred Astronomical Calendar
Of
Ancient Mexico

As
Its
Exacting catalyst,
And
Defining
A number of check points
Within its
1144 year periods,
It formulated
A prophecy
Unlike any other prophecy
Of mankind.
Its matrix
Lay hidden
In the shadows
Of
The lowland jungles,
All but
Lost in time,
Save
For the
Sacred Tablets
Held by the
Council of Quetzalcoatl.

These Tablets
prophecied
The coming events
Of the Americas,
Both
Land and people,
And did this
In a
Series of symbolic Heavens
Thirteen all told,
and
Nine Hells,
An accumulation

of twenty-two cycles
Of the
Fifty-two year calendar
Twenty-two times Fifty-two
Eleven hundred forty-four years.

The First Heaven
Had been entered
One hundred four years
Before
The birth
Of
The Lord of the Dawn.

In other words,
Two heavens
Had been spent
And the
First checkpoint
Had been
Arrived at
Upon the birth
Of the child
On the
Day One Reed
And the
Year One Reed.
This
Confirmed
In the minds
Of the believers
The accuracy
Of the prophecy

Ce Acatl is the Nahuatl name
For
One Reed.

Topiltzin is also a Nahuatl word
        Meaning
        Our Lord
        Or
        Our Prince,
        Thus,
        The child's calendar name
        Was
        "Ce Acatl Topiltzin Quetzalcoatl"
        In English
        "Our Lord One Reed Feathered Serpent"
        And He was
        The long-awaited
        Lord of the Dawn.

Ce Acatl's infancy was spent
        In the
        Temples of Xochicalco,
        Raised by
        The Temple Virgins,
        Loved and protected
        by all.

When he was quite young he
        Was taken
        To the
        Valley of the Moon
        Where
        He spent the rest
        Of his childhood,
        Returning to Xochicalco
        On occasion
        To take part in
        Holy days
        And certain ceremonies.

In the Valley of the Moon
        He played
        And lived
        The life
        Of any child.

Perhaps the only life
        He ever had
        That
        Really belonged
        To himself.
        There
        He realized
        The creation,
        The little brooks
        became
        His song
        And
        He talked
        To the old trees,
        Rolled in the deep grass
        And
        Whistled to the birds.

        He
        Became a friend
        To all the things
        Of
        The Valley of the Moon,
        Especially
        The Little People
        Who became
        His constant companions
        and
        One of them
        Known as Quill
        Became his teacher,
        Recalled to Ce Acatl
        The romance
        Of the Clouds and the Earth,
        Told him
        Of the
        Birth of life

And
Of the
Creation of the Little People,
Told him of
Two Lord and Two Lady
And
Their twins.
He asked if
Ce Acatl had a twin.
Ce Acatl said,
"Yes."
(But that's
another story)

Ce Acatl thought
Of the "Tree of Life"
And knew
Its importance
And
More than once
The thought
Came to him,
"How much alike
Is
The story of
The Clouds and the Earth,
And
My Mother and Father,
Only
The Earth didn't die."

He wondered
If
One day the Earth Mother
Would die,
And
His first prayer
At sunrise
Was always that
She wouldn't.

Salavi's death brought Ce Acatl
From the
Valley of the Moon.
He returned
To his valley
Many times,
But
only to visit.

Once Salavi was dead
Ce Acatl's life
Became
The property of
All of Mexico.

He
Was nine years old.

They say
He tore the mask
From
The Feathered Serpent
Of Xochicalco.

They say
He purified the
Story of Creation.

They say
He fasted twenty days
and
Spoke to the dead
Of Teotihuacan

They say
He went to Oaxaca
And
Talked to the Tree of Life.

They say
He met his twin
In Oaxaca.

They say
They, the twins,
meditated for forty days and nights.

They say
Their spiritual power
Was
So great
That
The womb of the Earth
Glowed for four years.

They say
He journeyed
To the World of the dead
To speak once more
With Salavi.

They say
Many things
Of this boy.
And
Always
Shall say even more.

Salavi was buried under
A
Tall spruce tree.
His flesh
Became a tear
Of
The Earth Mother,
Became
A spring.

And the spring
Is always
Known as
Charm Springs
And
Wanders all over
The earth.
Those
Who drink
Of its water
Will
Always be reminded
Of
Old Salavi,
A forerunner
of
The Lord of the Dawn.

THE MORNING STAR YOUTH

The Morning Star was
Bright in the heavens
When
Ce Acatl made
His decision
to go to the camp
Of the Chichimeca
And
Bring his father's bones back,
And to bury them
Beside
The grave of his mother.

So,
He went.

Mixcoatl's brother lured Ce Acatl,
who was now twenty years old,
On to a mountain top
To talk,
He said.
The brother
Was
A great warrior
And knew
He could
Kill
Ce Acatl
With
His bare hands.

Lightning flashed
From
The cloudless sky
And
The evil brother
Was hurled
Into the world of the dead.

.Ce Acatl
Returned to Xochicalco
With
His father's remains,
Dug the grave
Himself
Beside the grave
Of his mother,
Still marked
With the dead branch
Of
The ancient tree.

When
Mixcoatl's grave
Was closed
Ce Acatl
Said
A short prayer.
"There
Is no remover of difficulties
Other than
The Creator,
And
We all abide
By His bidding.
We
Are all his servants."
And
The dead branch
Turned green.

THE DIVINE RULER

Due to the death of Mixcoatl's brother,
Ce Acatl
Became the Emperor
Of the Chichimeca.

He first pacified them
With Hikuli
A divine cactus
With
No thorns.

"The cactus will not
Hurt you,"
He said,
"It has no thorns,

The cactus
Is a
Spirit medicine
That is meant
To bring back peace to your dreams,
Calm to your waking hours,
And
Purpose to your life!
Take it
And
Be reminded
That it is a part of
Your Earth Mother's spirit,
Not to be toyed with,
Not to be
Made
A god."

Tezcatlipoca and his secret society that
Now hid in shadows,
Waited
And laid their plans
For
The destruction of
Ce Acatl's
New
Way of life,
A
Sort of
Great Peace.

Now Ce Acatl called upon
The Nonoalca,
And
The Amanteca
At the Temple of Xochicalco.

The Nonoalca were of Zapotec,

Mazatec decent

And

The Amanteca were master artists,

Descendants of the Teotihuacan people

Who

In their past had built

The Pyramids of the Sun

And

The Moon,

And designed

The Temple of Butterflies

On the

Road of the Dead

In Teotihuacan

And

Had   covered

The Temple of the Butterflies

With images

Of the Little People.

The Nonoalca

Were

Mathematicians,

Philosophers

And Astronomers,

They had also

Mastered the

Art of casting gold.

Combining the skill of these ancient cultured people

With the vitality

Of the Chichimeca

Ce Acatl

Brought into clear focus

A new renaissance

Which flowered into

The

Jewel of Ancient Mexico

And
It's heart
Was in the
City of Wonder
Known as
Tollan.
The people
of Tollan
Became known as
The Toltec.

Tollan was the capital of the empire
Of empires.
Seldom, if ever,
Rivaled
In the world.
Tollan
Was the heart
Of all
That had ever been
Good and pure
In
This ancient land.
It was the
Essence of grandeur,
The apex of prosperity.
Tollan
Was pure spirit
Manifested
In works of stone and feather,
gold and jade.
It was a world
Of religious splendor
And
Godly fulfillment.
A sample
Of
What man
Could do

With
Peace.

They say
Corn grew the size of a man,
Each cob the size of a man.

They say
Cotton grew in many colors,
Red, green, blue, violet, turquoise
and Yellow,
Earth colors of tan, black, brown
And a pale orange.

They say
Fountains of pure water
Flowed through the city
And
That this water
Was brought from the
Very heart
Of the Earth.
They say
Cocoa trees grew throughout the city,
Vines of orchids
And vanilla, avocado and mangoes.

They say
Birds of many colors
And sizes
Lived
With the people of Tollan.

They say
The people of Tollan
Were
The most beautiful people
In all the world,
Because of what

They had done,
Because
They had learned
The secret of
Peace was:
The unity of all things.

But strangely
They began to
Forget What
They had been taught.
They say this was the
secret work of Tezcatlipoca
and the Jaguar societies,

They say,
The Toltecs,
The people of Tollan
Believing lies
Made a toy
Of the thornless cactus,
The Hikuli
And
Used it
As the sacrament
Of their God
Tezcatlipoca.

TEZCATLIPOCA
And The Changing Of The Sacred Cactus

In the olden days,
        In the days before
        The beginning
        Of the
        Thirteen Heavens,
        Tezcatlipoca
        Was not
        An evil god.
        According to stories,
        He once ruled the
        People of the Earth.
        He
        Was
        The Lord of Fire,
        And
        Prince of feasts.
        He
        Ruled the night sky,
        Thus
        He was known
        As the
        "Dark Lord of the North."

Long, Long ago he had been
        A Gifted One,
        They say
        He had come to Earth
        Directly from
        The Creator,
        And,
        Here on Earth
        He had done
        Many wonderful things.
        When he left
        He told the people

Of a new and wonderful prophet
That would come and visit them
He told them,
When that day comes
They should listen to the New Words.

Through the endless times that followed
His philosophy
Of Peace
And
Of Love
Lost its place in the
Minds of men.
His potency was gone,
His philosophy forgotten,
His purpose in coming changed,
Changed
To meet the desires of men,
Rather than
The desires of the Creator.

Now, with the Chichimeca,
He was reduced
To
The size of a
Bloodthirsty monster,
Who
Devoured human Hearts,
And
Destroyed stars in the sky
So
The Sun
Would not have to
Fight
With them
At Sunrise.

As surely as the ignorance of man
Was reflected

Upon the
Once beautiful philosophy
Of Tezcatlipoca,
So
Was it reflected upon
The once sensible
Use of Hikuli.

Hikuli was once the
Holy Sacrament
Of a Gifted One.
Its story goes back
Long, long before
Tezcatlipoca.
It was still the
Sacred brew of the
Temples
At the time
Of the Chichimeca migration
Into the
Valley of Mexico.

Now, it was used by fools,
Who thought
They could rule
The minds of man,
Thus
Rule the Earth.

Hikuli
Became the blinding light
That
Led the victims
To the top of the pyramid
To have their hearts
Ripped from their bodies,
In a horrible ceremony
Dedicated to
Tezcatlipoca.

Tezcatlipoca grew very large, very fast.
Now,
The Toltec,
The "new people",
Had everything,
And
Wanted more.
They
Scorned
The teachings of
Ce Acatl
Scorned the presence
Of the Nonoalca
And
The Amanteca.

The "New People" became drunk and conceited
With power and glory.
They
Brought forth images
Of their
Dark Lord
Of human sacrifice,
Tezcatlipoca,
And
Slowly began
To build the
Nightmare of the future,
War. . . ,
Conquest. . .,
And Gods.

THE FALL OF TOLLAN

Tollan started to crack
  And decay
  From within.
  Grim
  Were the faces
  Of the Nonoalca,
  Who
  Knew the prophecy
  Of
  The Lord of the Dawn.

"Now we will see our work,
  Our labor
  Wasted,"

  They said.
  "It is not wasted,"
  Said Ce Acatl,
  "You will see,
  Not one drop of sweat
  Was wasted here.
  You and I and
  The Toltec
  Have made something known here
  At Tollan.
  But, now,
  Our work is done. . . .
  Well, almost done.

One last gift I have for you
  Before I leave. . . ,"
  He said to
  The Toltecs.
  "At noon tomorrow
  Come to
  My Temple
  And
  I will give it to you.

Bring
Tezcatlipoca
So he may
Take part in
This
Gift of Gifts."

At noon of the next day
　　　The Toltecs
　　　Swarmed around
　　　Ce Acatl's
　　　Temple.
　　　So used were they
　　　To
　　　Receiving
　　　That they
　　　Had come to think
　　　It common,
　　　Rather than
　　　A gift.
　　　Many jeers came from the crowd,
　　　Laughter
　　　And mockery.

At the foot of Ce Acatl's Temple
　　　Was placed
　　　A great image of
　　　Tezcatlipoca,
　　　The Dark Lord of the North.

Ce Acatl Topiltzin Quetzalcoatl
　　　Walked down
　　　The great steps of
　　　The pyramid
　　　To the
　　　Stone statute of
　　　Tezcatlipoca.
　　　He smiled and said,
　　　"My Brother!

And you,
The Toltec,
You are also
My brothers and
My sisters."

Now, a hush fell over the crowd,
The sun
Seemed
To dim
In the sky.

"Fear not," said Ce Acatl.
"No harm will come
To you
This day.
You
Are as safe as
If in my Mother's homeland.
You cannot even hurt
Yourself
At this moment.

My people," he continued,
"You,
Wonderful,
Wonderful
Children.
I love you.
You are surely
The soul of the Earth.
You have not
Failed me in one way,
Nor
Will you ever.
Understand
What I am saying here,
For that is of importance.
Understand,
I did not try to be

Your Lord,
Nor
Did you try to be my people,
Nor
Did we try to build Tollan.
Understand
That all of this is senseless
Unless
It serves a greater purpose.

One day, a long time from now
In the days of
The Seventh Hell
A man
Or a boy
Or a woman
Or a girl
Will come to you
And
They will say,
'Behold the Tree of Life,'
Because
As surely as you cast me out
Of your city with scorn,
You may not
Cast out the
'Tree of Life.'

Ce Acatl then held up a large Hikuli
In his right hand.
With his foot
He dug a small hole
In the Earth.
"Now, watch," he said,
as he placed
The cactus
In the hole.
He stepped back

and
Looking at the sun
He spoke these words.
"Lord of the Dawn
Royal Seal of Eternal Life
Caster of Truths
Master of Cosmic Force
Creator of Time and Light
Giver of matter,
Touch this place."

He turned and walked back
Up the stairs
Of the pyramid.
"Fake!"
Someone shouted.
"Fake!
Liar
Sinner
Fake! "
Eater of filth
Devourer of human hearts,
Fake
Sinner
Liar
Eater of human flesh
Liar
Fake
Eater of human hearts
Devourer of human flesh."

But Hikuli became bitter,
So foul was it
That it made
People vomit.
No longer was it
A
Pleasant food.

Its name was now

    Peyote

    And

    It was like

    An uncontrollable Father,

    A Dark God.

    Cotton

    Grew in white only,

    Corn was corn only,

    White and yellow and sweet.

    The fountains went dry.

    The orchids

    Could not be grown,

    nor vanilla,

    Nor avocado,

    Nor mangoes.

    The

    Birds left.

And where Ce Acatl had placed

    The Hikuli

    a

    Tree of Thorns grew,

    And

    The strange forbidding tree

    Refused to die,

    It was created out of man's desire,

    And

    Insisted on living.

    All the cocoa trees

    Of Tollan

    Turned into

    Beautiful Thorn Bushes.

But the People, the Toltec, had
        What they wanted.
        They had
        Tezcatlipoca,
        The god of
        Human sacrifice.
        And Tezcatlipoca would write
        The history
        Of the Toltec
        And
        The people
        To follow the Toltec.

But at the end of the Ninth Hell
        Tezcatlipoca
        Would take off his mask
        And
        They would be surprised
        To learn
        Who he really is.

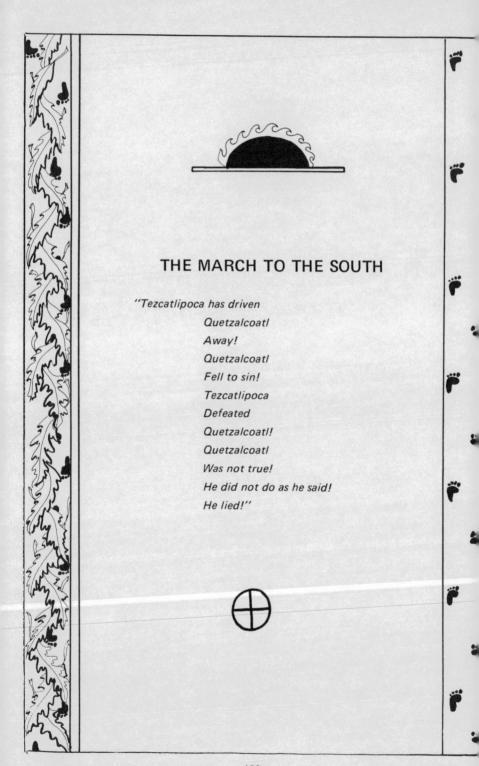

THE MARCH TO THE SOUTH

"Tezcatlipoca has driven
> *Quetzalcoatl*
> *Away!*
> *Quetzalcoatl*
> *Fell to sin!*
> *Tezcatlipoca*
> *Defeated*
> *Quetzalcoatl!*
> *Quetzalcoatl*
> *Was not true!*
> *He did not do as he said!*
> *He lied!"*

Those were the words
>Of the Toltec lords
>Who followed
>Ce Acatl,
>But,
>In the Sacred Temple
>Of Chamala,
>in Tollan,
>Some people,
>From time to time, came,
>And,
>Looking up at the
>Feathered Serpent on the wall,
>All that was left
>Of His sign at Tollan,
>They would pray.
>They would say
>*"Forgive!"*

Ce Acatl and his Nonoalca and Amanteca followers
>had left Tollan
>And traveled south.
>They
>Reached
>The valley of Mexico
>And
>Lake
>Tezcoco
>Where
>long ago
>The lovely Chimalma
>Had
>Received the Seed.
>Ce Acatl stopped there
>For many days
>And prayed.

Then on they went to the foot
Of the great Volcano,
To the famous
Popocatepetl.
There
His followers stopped
And
Made camp for awhile.
This
Was regarded
As the golden days
To Ce Acatl.

While he was there he told
The children
Many stories
At night,
By the blazing fire.
Told them stories
Of the
"Little People"
And
of Quill his
Pockwatchie teacher
And
Recalled many dreams
He had,
Long ago
In the
Valley of the Moon.

Here at the foot of the great volcano
Ce Acatl
roamed
Through the hills.
Once again
He sang with the brook
And whistled
To the bird,
Rolled in the deep grass

And returned for a moment
To the love of his childhood.

It is said that Quill returned to him
And that
The two of them
Smoked tobacco together
At an old pine tree stump
and Laughed
About the olden days.

Ce Acatl found these days to be sweet
As honey
And
Filled
With a thousand memories
He
Had forgotten
During
The sacrifice of Tollan.

The fresh snow water
And the
Clear mountain air
Was good for the whole tribe.
Deer meat
And
Autumn mushrooms,
Berries from the hollows,
And the
Fragrance of juniper fires
Transformed the camp-sight
into a natural shrine
Of human friendship.
Ce Acatl commented
That the glories of Tollan
Could never compare
With the least of the Creator's
wild lands,

And he said,
"The wealth that men die for
If only they knew,
Is but the corruptions
Of their own creations.
The real gift,
The gift a child can
Accept and love,
These solitudes of nature
With those you love,
Are as close as man
Can come to
What
He has in
His master plan."

Popocatepetl now loomed up before them.
Threatening smoke belched
From the mountain crater
And
Low rumbles came from the living stone.
The earth trembled
As the tribe climbed between
Popocatepetl and Ixtaccihuatl (the
Sleeping Lady) following a
prophecy,
Upward through the dense forest
Of the ever steepening slopes
Of the volcano.

More than two thirds of the tribe
was lost on the Mountain.
Fell to a blinding snow storm
High above the timber line,

Some
Were caught in
An avalanche
And swept away.

Others
Froze to death
During
The fireless nights
On the
Volcano of Death.
In a glen on the eastern slope
Of the mountain
Ce Acatl
At last sat
And wept
For
His lost companions,
He fasted
And meditated,
Prayed
And offered votives
In
Their memories.
Four
Men
Wandered into the camp
In this glen
And stayed awhile.
To talk.
These
Were four Holy Men
From
Four different directions.
Ce Acatl
Seemed to know them.
Each man spent
A day
In solitude with
Ce Acatl.
At the end
Of the fourth day
Ce Acatl
Called the

remaining of the tribe
Together
And with the
Four Holy Men
He told them
What
Had happened
And
What this meant.

"It was prophecied," he started,
"That these
Four men
Would find us here.
They are all
Holy Men.
All four of them
Know
Who they are
And
Why
They are here.

I have given each of them
Four words
To
Take Back
To their peoples
And to
put into
Their ceremonies
So
It will not be forgotten.

But one of these four words
Were commonly given
To each
Of the Holy Men.

I
Give
That Word
To
All of you now,
The word is
'Tree'.
Use it.
By the sign of the Tree
You
Will know
Each
And
Every
Manifestation
In this world.
All
Manifestations
are good,
None
Better than the other,
All
Are related
All
Are meant
To do
A part of
The Master Work.
Do not look
For miracles,
They will come.
Look
For the 'Tree'
And
Never,
Never
Forget it.

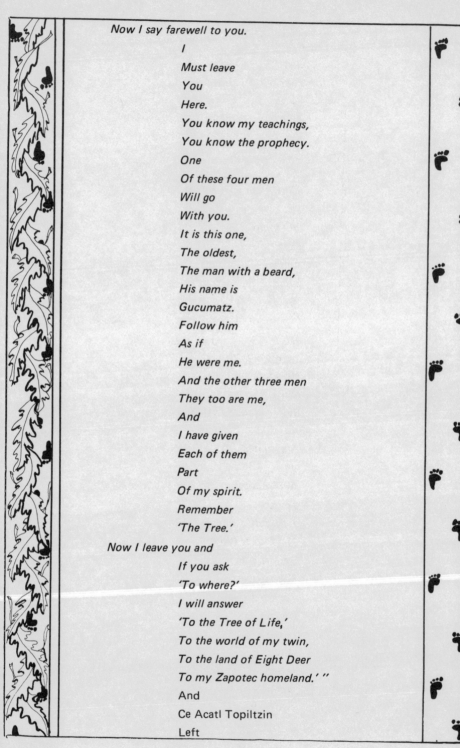

Now I say farewell to you.

I
Must leave
You
Here.
You know my teachings,
You know the prophecy.
One
Of these four men
Will go
With you.
It is this one,
The oldest,
The man with a beard,
His name is
Gucumatz.
Follow him
As if
He were me.
And the other three men
They too are me,
And
I have given
Each of them
Part
Of my spirit.
Remember
'The Tree.'

Now I leave you and
If you ask
'To where?'
I will answer
'To the Tree of Life,'
To the world of my twin,
To the land of Eight Deer
To my Zapotec homeland.' "
And
Ce Acatl Topiltzin
Left

And went to
Oaxaca,
To
The Valley of the Tree.

THE VALLEY OF THE TREE

During a terrible thunderstorm
It is said
Ce Acatl
Spent a night
With a
Huiteca family.
They fed him
And
Played music for him.
The father,
A strong Indian farmer
Showed Ce Acatl

A stone carving
He had and
Told him:

"This carving
Tells of
The coming of the
Lord of the Dawn.
It says
He will come
In the
Year One Reed.
It says
He will build a city
and
Change the world."

The farmer had no idea who
He was talking to.
He continued.
"Now," he said,
"Many people say
He will not come.
Many people say
It is a long time from now
That he will come.
Some people say
He will come from the East
And
He will bring a great book
Of words and numbers.
Other people say
He will come
From a tree
And
Count the
Last Twenty days
Of the Creation.

What
Do you say
About this?"

Ce Acatl grew grey with the depth
of his answer.
"If
I told you
Of my thought,
Of what I know
Of the Spirit
Of the Lord of the Dawn,
If I told you
Of what
I think will happen.
You would laugh
And think me crazy.

"So I say this only:
One day
A race
Shall walk upon this earth,
A race of men
Whose spirits
Are so great,
Whose wisdom
Is so complete,
Whose powers
To commune with the Creator
Are
So keen
They will dwarf
The doings
Of
The Lord of the Dawn
Of our day.
When that day comes
The Creator
Will send forth

A
Manifestation
That will
In turn
Amaze the wisest men
Of that
Unbelievable age.
And even then
The greatest brains on earth
Will wonder---
Has he come?
Will he come?
Or
Has he been here?"

In this way Ce Acatl traveled
          through the countryside.
          Meeting people,
          Staying overnight
          In their homes,
          Teaching
          And
          Leaving.
          Only to find another house,
          A village
          Or
          A lonely soul
          wandering through life alone

Till at last he reached the
          "Valley of the Tree."
          His sandals were worn out,
          His clothing bleached
          From the mountain sun
          His beard
          Had turned grey
          And
          His back
          Was growing weak,

He walked now
With a staff.

Through the valley he passed
    unnoticed
    As the
    Lord of the Dawn.
    Yet
    The thoughtful
    Zapotec people
    Made him feel
    Oaxaca
    Was his home.
    "Welcome old-man,"
    They said.
    "Welcome Grandfather!
    Eat and sleep,
    Rest and
    Tell us of your journey."

But Ce Acatl spoke not,
    And rested only
    At springs,
    Ate the food of the field
    And
    Carried On
    Toward the "great Tree"

Ce Acatl was forty-six when he reached
    The Valley of the Tree.
    This is not thought old
    In our time,
    But, in those days
    People died of old age
    At thirty-five
    And few lived to be forty.
    Most graves were of people
    Less than
    Twenty years of age.

It was late one evening
> When he at last
> Reached
> The Great Tree.
> He could see it
> For miles away
> And
> His approach
> Was slow.
> The Tree
> Seemed to glow
> With
> An ever brightening aura,
> Green in color
> Like transparent jade.

At last he reached the
> Great Tree,
> And fell
> Upon the roots,
> Exhausted.

There he slept and dreamed.
> When he awoke
> He found
> He
> Was surrounded
> By people,
> All of them
> Reflected holiness,
> All
> Were dressed in white,
> Wearing necklaces of clay
> Made
> In the form of
> The Circle
> And the Cross.

At last an old priest
Of their clan
Came forward.
"*I*
Know who you are,"
He said.
"*We*
Have been waiting for you."
Then
Very shyly he added:
"*Welcome!*
Welcome home my Lord!"
And like a burst of light
In a dark cave
The entire crowd
swarmed around him
And
Showered him
With such love as
He had never known before.

Everyone had to touch him
Or
He had to touch them.
Mothers
Brought their babies,
The
Children
Brought their dogs
And pet animals
And birds
For the
Lord of the Dawn to touch.
Laughter and excitement resounded
Through the Valley.
Dancing
And singing,
And merriment
Were
Everywhere.

The celebration went on
   For days,
   Perhaps weeks.
   The
   Lord of the Dawn
   Had
   Come home.

"And my twin?" Ce Acatl asked.
   "Too late,
   Years ago he was sacrificed
   On the Sacred Mountain
   By
   The Jaguar Priests,
   He was sacrificed
   With his lover,
   Two Turquoise.
   He had traveled
   Into
   The Nine Hells
   And
   Brought back a
   Message
   Of the future.

   He
   was faithful
   to
   Your cause
   Till the end."
"Of course he was," said Ce Acatl,
   "But
   It is
   Our Cause!"

Ce Acatl was given the news
   Of the Nonoalca
   And Gucumatz.

They
Had built a
Great pyramid
At the town
Of Cholula,
Given the word
And left.
They
Had gone on to
Yucatan
And
Were now building
A
New
Tollan.
They called the place
Chichen-Itza.

And a whole new era is coming about.
A great confederacy
Of
All the Maya
And Toltec tribes
Is
Being formed.
They say
The confederacy
Is based on
The
Philosophy of
The "Tree."

"It is good to hear these words
Of Our Cause,"
Said Ce Acatl.
"But I have little time
Left to talk.
Time is running out,
My cycle will soon close,
And
We have our greatest work

Laid
Out for us."

Ce Acatl resigned himself
To live under
The ancient Tree
And to work from
The Tree.
For four years
He
Did so.
There, under the Tree,
He designed
The
Sacred Tree of Mitla,
And called it a
Library,
The House of Books.

"This," he said, "is a monument
To the Tree of Life,
To
The whole Creation.
The city
Will be like a Tree,
Half above the Earth,
Half below the Earth,
The trunk
And
The roots.

The roots will be the
Tombs of our dead.
The artist,
Poet,
Writers of books,
The Librarians
Who
Will be the

Great Seers
Readers of all books,
They too shall be
Tombed
In the roots.

As the roots of a tree reaches
Down into the past,
So
The roots of this Library,
Will Reach
Into its own past.
Mitla
Will be like
a
Stone Tree.

Above the surface
Will stand the temples,
The Library itself.
And it,
Like a tree,
Will reflect
What it
Has been subjected to
By the
Natural forces.

Wind rising, rain falling.
Sun rising, sun falling.
Clouds rising, lightning falling
Life rising, death falling
Tide rising, tide falling
Man rising, man falling.
Tree of Life rising, rising, rising."

The Library,
The house of books
Came to be

Exactly as
He
Had designed it.
It was built
At the
Womb of the Earth,
At the
Cave
Of the Nether World.

And the Temples of Mitla are unique
In the
World of
Architectural design,
The
Epitome
Of
Zapotec-Mixtec Art.
Every stone
Was cut
By human hands.
Perfectly in balance
With
All things,
And done by
People who
Knew that
This
Was far more
Than a building.

The question has often been asked,
Who
Built
The Temples of Mitla?

It was designed by the
                    Lord of the Dawn,
                    And built
                    By people
                    Who loved
                    And
                    Who followed
                    Him!

It was done, but Ce Acatl
                    Never saw
                    The Temple completed.
                    He had come
                    From the
                    Dawn of the Third Heaven
                    And
                    Stayed a while,
                    Stayed fifty-two years
                    And
                    Left.
                    Gone to his
                    Mother's homeland,
                    To the
                    Land of the Black and the Red.

He, Ce Acatl Topiltzin, had come
                    Out of the Black,
                    The darkness of
                    Man's mind,
                    entered into
                    The Red World of the Sun,
                    And had returned,
                    Knowing
                    More than all others
                    For
                    He had penetrated
                    The world of time and
                    Completed a cycle set forth

In another creation
long, long ago,
and far,
Ever so far away.

Four years he had spent under
The most ancient Tree.
There
He had designed the
Library,
At the
Womb of the Earth Mother.
Designed a Library
Like a
Sacred City
And that City
Became known as
Mitla,
City of the Dead.

Ce Acatl was fifty-two years old
When he died.
One short cycle
Of the Sacred Calendar,
One
Of the Lord of Life's
Thirteen Heavens
Was all the time
He
Was given.

The date of his birth by the Christian Calendar
Was
947 AD,
His departure
999AD.

FRUIT OF THE SACRED TREE

His death marked the beginning
of the
Fourth cycle.
The
Fourth Heaven.

The riddle of the Thirteen heavens
And
Nine Hells
Has challenged
The imagination
Of man

Since first it
Came to light.

With Ce Acatl's birth, part of the prophecy
Was realized
And became clearer
To the beholders.
His death
And the
Last prophecy
Before his death
Shattered
The minds
Of the most conscientious
Of men.

This is
How it happened
At the
"Tree of Life"
In the
Valley of Oaxaca.

Remember the four holy men
Who came to
His camp on
Popocatepetl,
How
He gave them
Each
Four words,
One word of which
Was common to them all.
That word was
"Tree",
He made this
Gift of words
in one day
To each man
Four holy men came
Four days he spent
Four words were given
Four directions were ordered.

One of the directions
Was that of
The Oldest Holy Man,
Gucumatz.
He,
Like the other three
Was given
A part of the
Lord of the Dawn's Spirit.
Each of them
Was now a

Lord of the Dawn,
Of Sorts.
Each
Was destined to
Fulfill a part
Of the
Lord of the Dawn's prophecy
And to
Make the "Tree" known
In their people's ceremonies,
And
To repeat
The prophecy of the
Thirteen Heavens
And
Nine Hells.

We read of Gucumatz,
The Holy Man
Who came among the Maya
And
Did the work
Of the Lord of the Dawn.

That story is mentioned
In the Sacred Book
Of the Quiche Mayan,
The Popol Vuh.
The record of
Gucumatz
Is well preserved
Because it survived
The destruction
of the end of the
Thirteen Heavens,
Few books survived
The Spanish Conquest
and therefore we have little
To go on

Regarding the
Founding of the ceremony
Of the Volador
Or
The Dance of the Xocatlhuetzi.

Here is a description
Of part of the
Xocatlhuetzi ceremony
Described by
Alfonso Caso
In His
Aztecs; People of the Sun,

"With much ceremony they brought this tree, called xocatl, from the forest, dancing and singing to it as if it were a god, carrying it upon other logs so that the bark would not be injured. When they drew near the city, the women of the nobility came out to receive them, with jugs of chocolate and with garlands of flowers which they hung upon the necks of the bearers."

And
Again from Caso's
Aztecs; People of the Sun.
The game of
The Volador.

* From *The Aztecs: People of the Sun,* by Alfonso Caso. © 1958 by the University of Oklahoma Press.

"Another sport that had religious significance was the game we know by the name of *volador.* It is still played by the Totonacs of the northern part of the state of Veracruz."

"This game required climbing a very tall, slick pole, near the top of which was fastened a square wooden frame. Each of the four players participating in this dangerous sport was tied to a corner of the framework. The four were dressed as macaws, birds sacred to the sun. A fifth individual stood atop the mast on a cylinder, which revolved as he played the flute. The four men tied to

146

the corners of the frame jumped off at the same time, so that the ropes to which they were tied would unreel and cause the wooden cylinder on which the flute player stood to turn around and around. Each player whirled around the pole thirteen times, and on the last revolution, as soon as his feet touched the ground, he began running. The four macaws jumping from the pole and whirling around it thirteen times are symbolic of the fifty-two years that make up the Aztec cycle of years, that is, the movement of the sun in the thirteen-multiplied-by-four revolutions which equal fifty-two years."

It is interesting
To note
The Volador game
Was known
As far north as
Taos in New Mexico
And is mentioned
By Frank Waters in
THE BOOK OF THE HOPI.
These verifications
Are from the south,
From Meso America.
Here are two verifications
From the north.
First,
From the Iroquois Prophet
Deganaweda
In founding the
Confederacy of the "Tree"

In 1571
We are told
He used these words:
"With the Five Confederate Lords
We plant this Tree of Peace
The roots of this tree
Will spread throughout the world.
We call these roots,
The White Roots of Peace.

* From *The Aztecs: People of the Sun,* by Alfonso Caso. © 1958 by the University of Oklahoma Press.

"Should any one, or any nation
Seek the protection of this Tree,
Let them follow the Roots to their source,
And take refuge with the People of the Earth."

In Black Elk's book the
Sacred Pipe,
He describes
The
Seven Sacred Rites
Of the Sioux.
One of which
Is the Sun Dance
And the
Building of the
Sun Dance Lodge.
The center pole,
The Sun Dance Pole
Is
The "Tree of Life."

It may well be said that
Black Elk's
Book of the
Sacred Pipe and
The Seven Sacred Rights of the Sioux
Is a
Ceremonial history
Of the
Manifestation
Of the
Lord of The Dawn
And of the
Thirteen Heavens
And
Nine Hells, for the Sioux
mention two circles

to
Come after
the
First Seven.

From the Huichol Indians of Nayarit
Come the God Eyes,
Those lovely little
Star-like votives
So popular today
Among
The southwestern people
Of the United States.

The God Eye is the
Symbol of children.
The God Eye itself
Represents the
Eye of God as
Seen through the
Vision
Of a child.

When the Huichol child is born
The umbilical cord
Is buried beneath
An old tree.
This tree
Is made known
To the
Child
As he grows.
It is called,
"Grandfather."

Two sticks are taken from the tree
And tied together
At the center,
In the form of a cross.
The yarn is woven

From
Stick to stick
Symbolizing
The growth of life.
The yarn

 Winds it's way
Toward
The end of the sticks,
When at last
The sticks
Have been covered,
Life has been spent,
The God's Eye
Is tied
To a low branch
Of the tree.
There the wind
Will blow it,
The birds
Will pick at it
And
The sun
Will bleach it.
In the end
it will return
To the Earth Mother
As all things must.

To the Huichols of Nayarit this simple ceremony
Symbolizes
The child
Coming from the
"Tree of Life"
And
Returning to his
Earth Mother
In the end.

The four disciples of
Ce Acatl

Did an excellent job.
Each
Accomplished
The work of a
Master Prophet,
A
Universal Teacher.
But
Ce Acatl
Had not finished.

The staggering blow to the ego
Of the non-believer
Came
In the form of
A miraculous prophecy
That
Literally shatters
The imagination
Of Modern man.

Upon his departure he vowed
To return
And close
The Thirteen Heavens
And to open
The Nine Hells.
He vowed
To destroy
The man-made gods
Of His people.
He set the day
Of his birth
And the year
Of his birth
As the time
To do
All of that.

The fifty-two year cycle was
  The Short Circle.
  Five short circles
  Equal
  A Full Circle,
  Or
  5 x 52 = 260.
  Every
  Two hundred and sixty years
  The day and year sign
  Of
  One Reed
  Would take place.
  Thus,
  He corrected the calendar
  And said:
  "On the Day One Reed,
  And
  The Year One Reed
  I shall return.
  I will come
  From the east
  Like the
  Morning Star
  And
  I will fulfill *that* part
  Of the
  Prophecy.

And Ce Acatl Topiltzin Quetzalcoatl,
  The
  Lord of the Dawn
  Departed
  Into the
  World of the Dead,
  To the Underworld,
  To Mitla.
  There he rested,

And
Waited,
And
Waited.

It is said the sun disappeared
From the sky
When
He passed.
It is said
The birds
Stopped singing
And that a
Hush fell
Over the entire planet.
And
Burning bright
In the heavens
Directly above
The great tree,
The Tree of Life,
Glowed
The planet Venus,
The
Morning Star.

The march to the south
Was done!

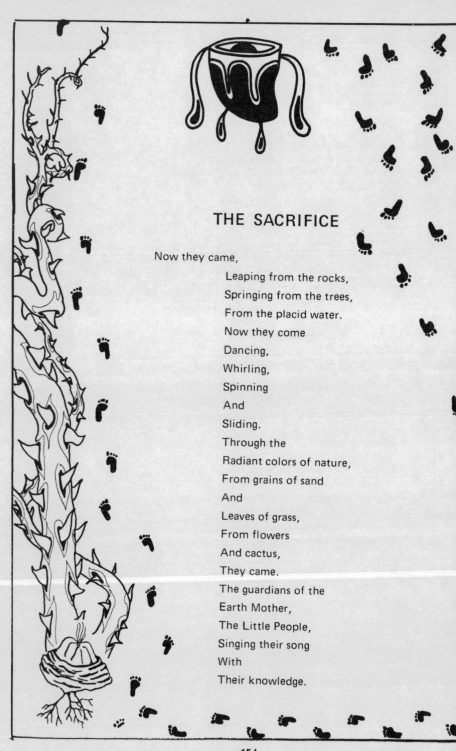

THE SACRIFICE

Now they came,

    Leaping from the rocks,

    Springing from the trees,

    From the placid water.

    Now they come

    Dancing,

    Whirling,

    Spinning

    And

    Sliding.

    Through the

    Radiant colors of nature,

    From grains of sand

    And

    Leaves of grass,

    From flowers

    And cactus,

    They came.

    The guardians of the

    Earth Mother,

    The Little People,

    Singing their song

    With

    Their knowledge.

Sad at first, with the parting
    Of their friend,
    But
    Quickly returning
    To joy
    With the realization
    Of what was coming.
    The greatest adventure
    Was
    Just beyond
    The horizon
    And the tiny
    Earth spirits knew
    It was there.

They watched the history unfold
    Before their little eyes.
    From their hiding places
    They saw,
    They heard,
    and
    They kept close count
    Of the
    Thirteen Heavens.

As had been prophesied
    They saw Tollan,
    The Emerald of Mexico
    Fall
    And
    Weather
    Like bones in the Sun.

And the Aztecs came,
    As wild nomads
    From the north.
    Came
    From the
    Same land

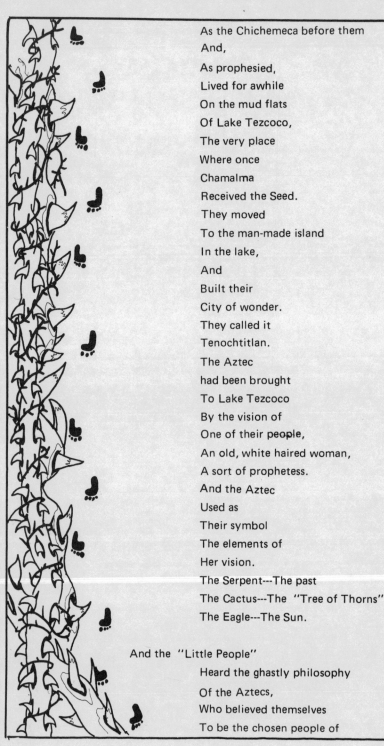

As the Chichemeca before them
And,

As prophesied,
Lived for awhile
On the mud flats
Of Lake Tezcoco,
The very place
Where once
Chamalma
Received the Seed.
They moved
To the man-made island
In the lake,
And
Built their
City of wonder.
They called it
Tenochtitlan.
The Aztec
had been brought
To Lake Tezcoco
By the vision of
One of their people,
An old, white haired woman,
A sort of prophetess.
And the Aztec
Used as
Their symbol
The elements of
Her vision.
The Serpent---The past
The Cactus---The "Tree of Thorns"
The Eagle---The Sun.

And the "Little People"
Heard the ghastly philosophy
Of the Aztecs,
Who believed themselves
To be the chosen people of

the Sun
And
Like all chosen people,
They became lost.
They believed
The Sun was God,
A great Eagle.

The Sun is a warrior,
            Said the Aztec Lord,
            The Sun must
            Fight the stars
            From the sky
            At every dawn.

We, the Aztec, are sent
            To Earth
            To feed the Sun,
            To strengthen him
            So He can continue
            His fight against
            The stars.

And the strengthening food,
            The all powerful substance
            That kept the Sun alive
            Was found
            In the human heart.
            The Curse of
            Tezcatlipoca.

But, even here the Morning Star
            Was
            The forerunner
            Of the Sun.

The tiny Earth spirits watched
            The happenings.
            They saw

The
Temples of Mitla
Finished
And knew what
They were designed
To do,
And what
They really meant.
They saw the Librarian,
The Great Seer,
Struggle to keep
The memory of the
Lord of the Dawn
Alive
And pure.

At Chichen Itza they saw
The rise
Of
The New Republic
Of the Tree,
Through the image
Of Kukulcan,
The Feathered Serpent,
Watched it fall
Like autumn leaves,
Decay
And return sadly
To Human Sacrifice,
In the
Name of
Quetzalcoatl!

In the Eighth Heaven it began,
And
By the Tenth Heaven
The Mayan Tree
Had grown thorns.

In the Eleventh Heaven
                    Some Mayans
                    Knew
                    What was happening,
                    The ones who
                    Had stayed in tune
                    With creation.

From D. G. Brinton's
                    "The Book of Chilam Balam"
                    The words fall
                    Like leaves
                    Of another autumn,
                    Reminiscent of the
                    Coming of the
                    Lord of the Dawn,
                    But this
                    came
                    nine cycles later.

"Eat, eat, while there is bread,
Drink, drink, while there is water;
A day comes when dust shall darken the air,
When a blight shall wither the land,
When a cloud shall arise,
When a mountain shall be lifted up,
When a strong man shall seize the city.
When ruin shall fall upon all things.
When the tender leaf shall be destroyed
When eyes shall be closed in death,
When there shall be three signs on a tree,
Father, son, and grandson hanging dead on
                    the same tree;
When the battle flag shall be raised,
And the people scattered abroad in the Forest."

And in the Twelfth Heaven
                    Among the Aztec came
                    This sad song,

A prayer,
A plea
Bitter
With the fruits
Of the
"Tree of Thorns."
"We only came to sleep,
We only came to dream,
It is not true, no, it is not true
That we came to live on the earth.

"We are changed into the grass of springtime;
Our hearts will grow green again
And they will open their petals,
But our body is like a rose tree:
It puts forth flowers and then withers."

The chosen people of the Sun,
The Aztec.
Had
Truly been chosen,
But
They knew not
What task lay before them.
Nor
Could they have dreamed
The scope
of the tragedy.

The thirteenth Heaven opened with
A swirl of confusion.
The entire planet
seemed to be engulfed
in some overwhelming restlessness.

The year on the Western Man's calendar
Was 1467 AD.
War and rebellion
raged throughout

the world.
Exploration,
Conquest lay
In the future of Europe.
New frontiers expanding
Across the surface
Of the Earth.

The population of Europe was exploding
At an unbelievable rate of speed,
And
The population wanted
Freedom
And liberty,
And justice.

Drought and epidemics,
Earthquakes
And land slides
Heralded
The coming of the
Prophetic fulfillment
In Mexico.

Drums of restlessness
echoed across
The entire continent.
Time
Had run out.
The Thirteenth Heaven
Was
About to close
And
Moctezuma
Was warned.
First
By his Astrological priesthood,
Then
By

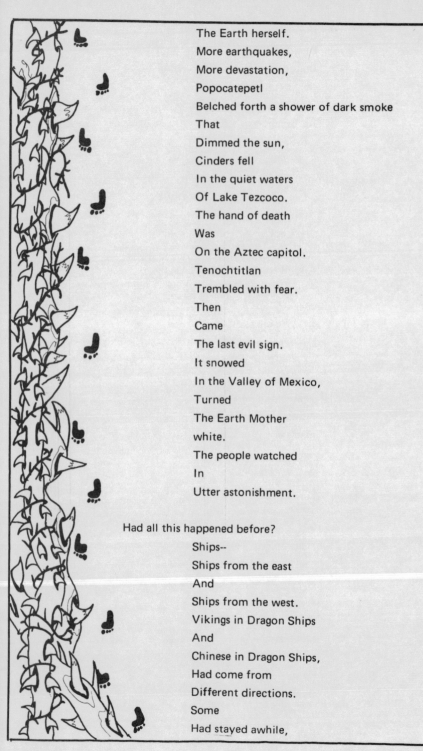

The Earth herself.
More earthquakes,
More devastation,
Popocatepetl
Belched forth a shower of dark smoke
That
Dimmed the sun,
Cinders fell
In the quiet waters
Of Lake Tezcoco.
The hand of death
Was
On the Aztec capitol.
Tenochtitlan
Trembled with fear.
Then
Came
The last evil sign.
It snowed
In the Valley of Mexico,
Turned
The Earth Mother
white.
The people watched
In
Utter astonishment.

Had all this happened before?
Ships--
Ships from the east
And
Ships from the west.
Vikings in Dragon Ships
And
Chinese in Dragon Ships,
Had come from
Different directions.
Some
Had stayed awhile,

Some never left,
Some disappeared.
But
None of them
Changed the ancient prophesy,
The fifty-two year cycles
Continued to count away
The minutes,
Days
And years
Of the
Thirteen Heavens
And the
Nine Hells.
No Viking,
No Chinese
Had changed that pattern,
They, in turn,
Stayed or
Left in astonishment.

The Morning Star had cleared
The horizon of
The Great Eastern Sea.
The place
Was known as
The True Cross,
Veracruz today.
And as the
Morning Star
Rose in the sky
The sun started to show
Its light
Revealing the sails
Of ships.
Ships
With great crosses
Painted on them,
Ships with men

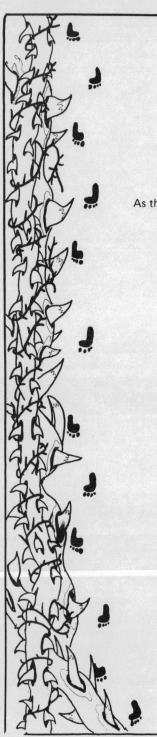

In shining metal armour,
Ships
With cannons
And swords
Ships
With horses and saddles,
Great ships
Loaded
With disease.
As the small rowboats
were detached
From the great ships
And started for shore
Their leader asked a question
Of the Catholic Priest
Who sat beside him:
"What is today?"
He asked.
"Good Friday; Senor Cortez,"
The priest answered.
"I know that,
I mean what is the date?"
Cortez said.
"April 21st, 1519,
Senor Cortez,
Have you forgotten?"
"No," said Cortez;
"I didn't forget,
I wondered
If anyone else remembered.
This
Is a Very important day."

"On the Day One Reed
            and
The Year One Reed
I shall Return.
I will come from
      the east
Like the Morning
            Star" ...... Quetzalcoatl

Revelation Chapter 22:16
                I, Jesus have sent mine angel
                to testify unto you these things
                in the churches.
                I am the root
                And the offspring of David,
                And
                The bright and Morning Star.

The Year One Reed
The Day One Reed, had come.

LORD OF THE NINE HELLS

Rivers of tears flowed

Through Mexico

Rivers of blood flowed

From

The Heart of the Earth.

Rivers of sorrow,

Rivers of pain,

"Oh, My God, thy water of precious stones

Has fallen

The tall cypress

Has changed into a quetzal bird

The fire serpent

Has been changed into a plumed serpent."

Tenochtitlan had fallen,

Moctezuma was dead,

The Aztec empire fell

Like an aspen leaf

In the mountain breeze

And

Sunk

To the bottom of Lake Tezcoco.

The prophecy of the Lord of the Dawn

Had been completed.

In Oaxaca,

At Mitla,

Not far from

The Tree of Life,

The young Mixtec Priest spoke,

His voice calm,

Assured

That he knew what

Was really happening.

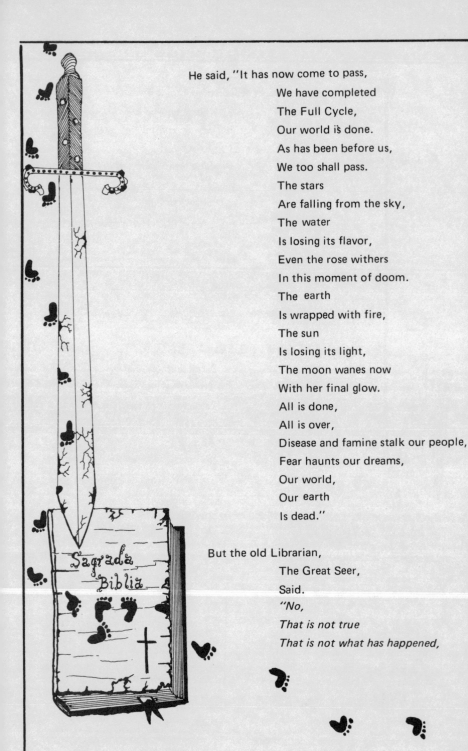

He said, "It has now come to pass,
We have completed
The Full Cycle,
Our world is done.
As has been before us,
We too shall pass.
The stars
Are falling from the sky,
The water
Is losing its flavor,
Even the rose withers
In this moment of doom.
The earth
Is wrapped with fire,
The sun
Is losing its light,
The moon wanes now
With her final glow.
All is done,
All is over,
Disease and famine stalk our people,
Fear haunts our dreams,
Our world,
Our earth
Is dead."

But the old Librarian,
The Great Seer,
Said.
"No,
That is not true
That is not what has happened,

And that
Is not the way it is going to happen.
This
Is the way
It really is, He said.
We have lived
Through thirteen heavens.
Thirteen cycles of fifty-two year epics.
For the first heaven
We were
Pure and simple.
We knew nothing
And
We doubted nothing.
The gifts
Of our Earth Mother
Belonged to all who lived.
The gifts
Were ours
For the taking.
But,
We
Made them complex.
We
Put a value of exchange

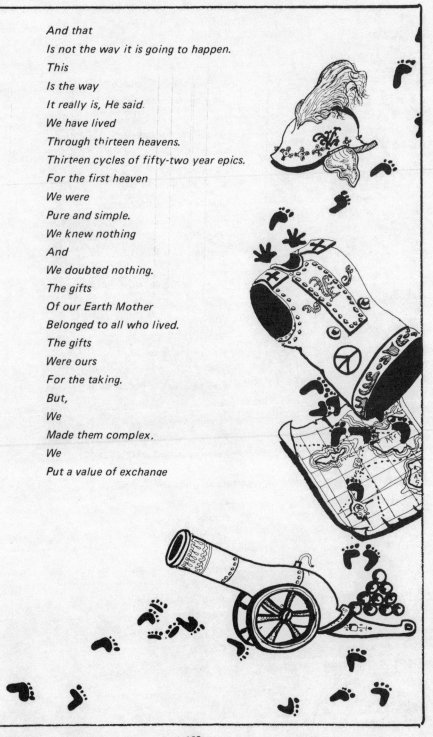

To them
And
Each heaven thereafter
Became more restrictive,
We
Became more involved
With
Our own creations
Rather than with
Our Earth Mother
And
Her gifts.
She has not changed,
She
Is the same beautiful sphere
That
She was in the beginning
Her gifts
Still spring from her flesh,
She
Still gives all to her children.
We
Have changed.
Perhaps not all of us have changed,
Perhaps not all of us have forgotten.

We have ended the Thirteen Heavens,
We will now
Enter
The Nine Hells,
Now
Things will change.

Foreign lords with foreign gods
Have come
With greater power.
They,
Understand nothing about us,

Nor
Do they really desire
To
Know our stories,
Our histories.
They
Will impose
Their way
Upon us
And
We will hear them,
And
Believe them
Or
We will die.
Many of us will die anyway,
It matters little
What we believe.
We
Will grow our crops
For them,
Toil in the field
For them.
Sweat in the shops
For them.
We
Will forsake our Gods,
For them.
Their holy men,
Their sacred books,
Their prophecies
Shall prevail.
Ours
Will be thought the prattle of children,
Our temples
Will give way
To theirs,
Our altars
Will be replaced

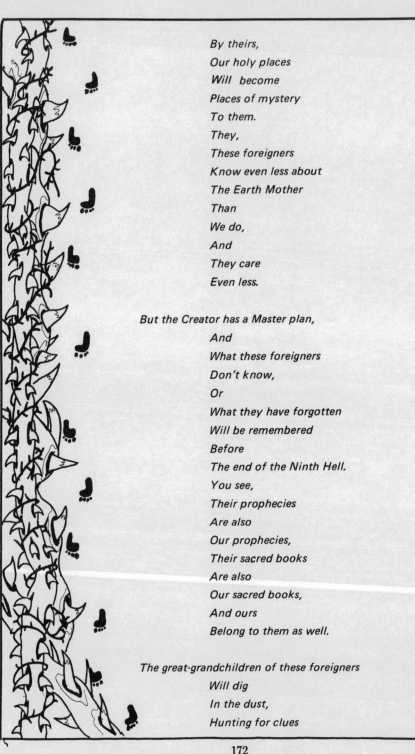

By theirs,
Our holy places
Will   become
Places of mystery
To them.
They,
These foreigners
Know even less about
The Earth Mother
Than
We do,
And
They care
Even less.

But the Creator has a Master plan,
And
What these foreigners
Don't know,
Or
What they have forgotten
Will be remembered
Before
The end of the Ninth Hell.
You see,
Their prophecies
Are also
Our prophecies,
Their sacred books
Are also
Our sacred books,
And ours
Belong to them as well.

The great-grandchildren of these foreigners
Will dig
In the dust,
Hunting for clues

To
What we are,
What is now
Being destroyed.

Prepare yourself for death
    My
    Young men and women
    Of the Order of the
    Lord of The Dawn,
    Because
    The Lord of the Nine Hells
    Has come,
    His name is Tezcatlipoca.''

The population of Mexico
    Between the Isthmus of Tehuantepec
    And the
    Valley of Mexico
    Is estimated at between
    Twenty and twenty-eight million
    People
    At the time of the conquest.
    One Hell later,
    Fifty-two years
    From the time
    Cortez landed at Veracruz
    The population
    Of that part of Mexico
    Was
    Reduced
    To less than one million people.

The end did not come
    With the Spanish Conquest
    For the Spaniard,
    Like the Pilgrim Fathers,
    And the founders of Jamestown,
    Was

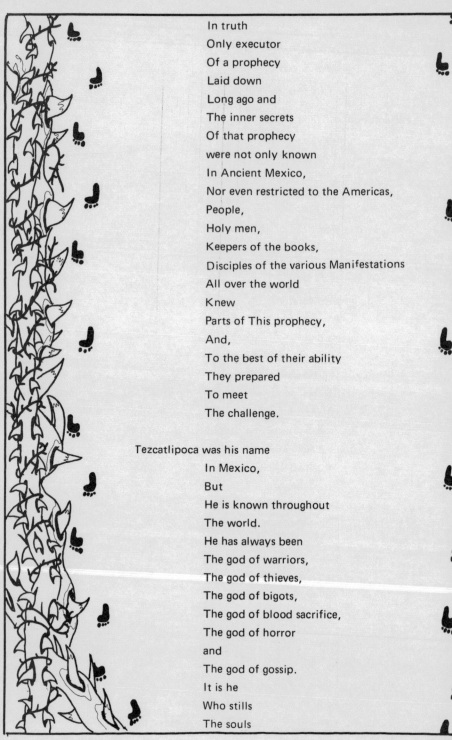

In truth
Only executor
Of a prophecy
Laid down
Long ago and
The inner secrets
Of that prophecy
were not only known
In Ancient Mexico,
Nor even restricted to the Americas,
People,
Holy men,
Keepers of the books,
Disciples of the various Manifestations
All over the world
Knew
Parts of This prophecy,
And,
To the best of their ability
They prepared
To meet
The challenge.

Tezcatlipoca was his name
In Mexico,
But
He is known throughout
The world.
He has always been
The god of warriors,
The god of thieves,
The god of bigots,
The god of blood sacrifice,
The god of horror
and
The god of gossip.
It is he
Who stills
The souls

Of those
Who follow him.

The philosophy of Tezcatlipoca
    Is exemplified
    In this quotation
    From
    Alfonso Casos'
    Aztecs; People of the Sun.

"Since he was young, he was the first to arrive
at the festivities when the gods returned, in
the month of Teotleco. He carried off old
Tlaloc's wife, Xochiquetzal, goddess of flowers
and love, of whom he said:

"I believe that she is truly a goddess,
That she is really very beautiful and fine.
I shall have her, not tomorrow, nor the
next day, nor the next, but right now, at
this moment, for I, in person, am he who
ordains and commands it so. I am the
Young Warrior who shines like the sun and has
The beauty of the dawn."

* From *The Aztecs: People of
the Sun,* by Alfonso Caso.
© 1958 by the University of
Oklahoma Press.

The philosophy of Tezcatlipoca
    Is direct and
    Without flowery phrases.
    Rape,
    Murder,
    Steal,
    Lie,
    Control,
    Torture,
    He with the greater club
    Is right,
    He with no club
    Toils.

And those holy men,
>The keepers-of-the-book
>Knew
>That on April 21, 1519 AD
>It
>Was not
>The coming of Tezcatlipoca,
>It
>Was in truth
>The day he started to work.
>He is a great master,
>He wears a strange mask
>And before
>The end of the Ninth Hell
>He will
>Take it off
>And all of us
>Will be surprised
>Who
>He
>Really is.

"THE REQUIEM"
the Mass celebrated for
the repose of the souls of
the dead. . . .

Webster's Dictionary

THE REQUIEM

The Little People, the Tlaloques and Pockwatchies
Watched on.
They saw
The dark shadow fall
Across the lands.
Saw the battles fought,
The drums silenced,
Saw
The Father,
Son,
And Grandson
Hang from the same tree.
Watched the railways
Span the plains,
Saw the buffalo disappear,
The tribes
Herded like cattle
Onto reservations.
Heard the newborn babies cry
And
Saw them buried

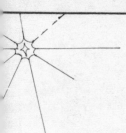

In lonely frozen graves
Far
From their original homes.
Heard
The death song
Of
Crazy Horse.
Saw
Sitting Bull
murdered,
The Ghost Dance
Rise and fall
And
Father Peyote
Attempt a return,
And fail.

And they were the witness to
The Rivers of filth,
Destruction of forests,
Devastation of land,
Pollution of lakes,
They saw
The springs disappear,
Like hidden tears.
And
They mourned
The
Untimely decay
Of
Their Earth Mother.
They saw
The tender leaf destroyed
And
The mountain lifted up,
The canyons filled in.
They saw
The cities rise

And
Watched
The smoke settle
And
Heard
The groan
Of a people in despair.

The Little People knew
What was happening,
But
They could not stop it,
And
They knew that.

The atom bomb is by all means
The
Greatest destroying force
Ever used by man
Against
Man.

It is the energy of the
Sun
Trapped
On earth.

When the first test was made
At
White Sands, New Mexico
July 16, 1945,
The scientists
Gasped
At the power
They
Now held in their hands.

According to the prophecy
We

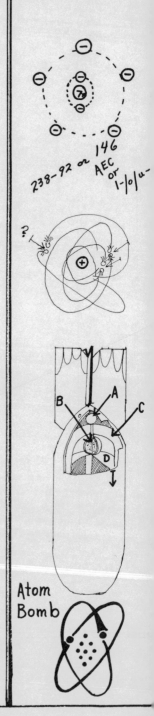

Entered the ninth hell
On
August 3, 1935.
In
March of that year
Adolph Hitler
Startled the world
When
He denounced the clauses
Of the
Versailles Treaty
Providing for
German disarmament.

The swastica, with its chosen superman philosophy,
Had
Started to rise.
And,
As with the Aztecs before them,
The Germans
Used the slogan
"We are the Super-race,
The chosen people,
Set forth to justify
The wrongs of man,
We are all wise,
All sound,
All intelligent,
We
Will rule,
Today Berlin,
Tomorrow the world."

"Today Tenochtitlan, tomorrow the world
     And our god
     Is the
     Sun,"
     Said the Aztec.

Ten years and three days
     After
     We entered
     The Ninth Hell,
     On August 6, 1945,
     The first
     Atom bomb was dropped
     On
     Hiroshima, Japan.
     The world
     was stunned
     When
     Three days later
     On
     August 9, 1945,
     The second bomb
     Struck
     Nagasaki.
     The
     Power of the Sun-god
     On Earth!

It is interesting to note that
     The atom bomb
     was assembled
     At
     Los Alamos, New Mexico.
     Los Alamos is
     The
     Spanish name
     For
     Cottonwood Tree.

The war is over! some said.
But,
Is it
Really over.
Was the
Second World War
In truth
The opening of the Ninth Hell.
The world
Has
Not felt rest,
Realized peace
Since that horrible date ?
In August of 1935.
Mounting tensions,
Religious decay,
Mass confusion,
War,
Strife,
And intrigue
Has brought
All people
To
An awareness
That
Something is happening,
Something
We cannot control.

Racial identity, Youth identity,
Racial and youth rebellion,
Followed by
An international explosion
Of
Drug addiction
Moral and political decay,
Rape,
Murder,
Robbery
Are common words among
Our third grade Americans.

The Philosophy of
Tezcatlipoca.

Is God dead?
What is happening
To our children?
Will
This Hell
Ever end?

Yes!
It will end on
August 16, 1987.

What will happen then?
Will all of this
Be
destroyed,
Will the earth
Be
Blown up
And
All of this be
Lost,
What   will happen?

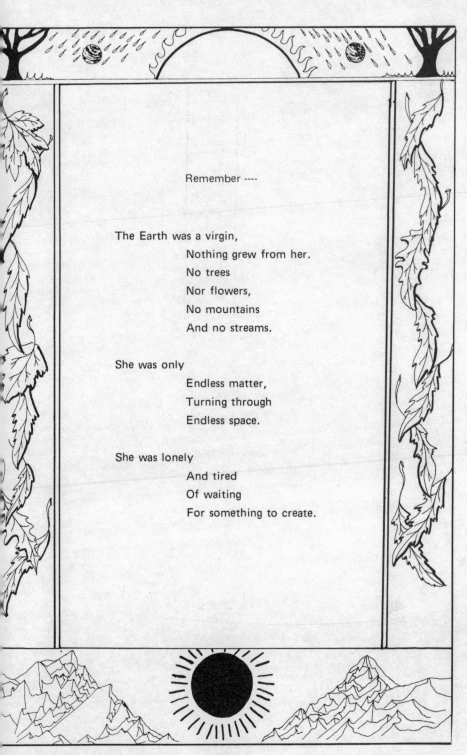

Remember ----

The Earth was a virgin,
Nothing grew from her.
No trees
Nor flowers,
No mountains
And no streams.

She was only
Endless matter,
Turning through
Endless space.

She was lonely
And tired
Of waiting
For something to create.

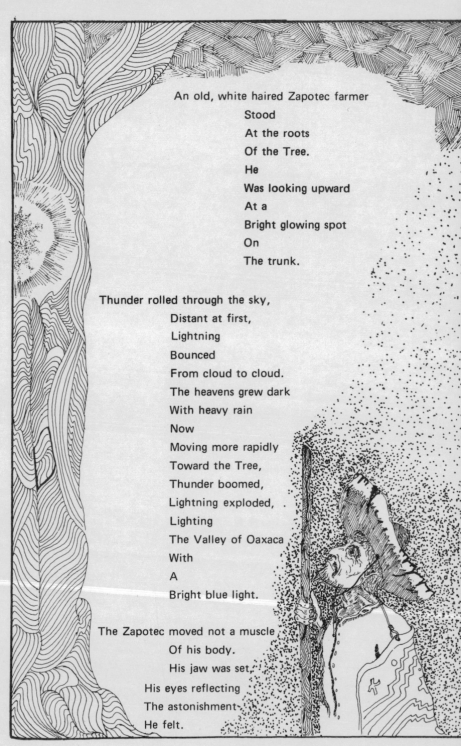

An old, white haired Zapotec farmer
    Stood
    At the roots
    Of the Tree.
    He
    Was looking upward
    At a
    Bright glowing spot
    On
    The trunk.

Thunder rolled through the sky,
    Distant at first,
    Lightning
    Bounced
    From cloud to cloud.
    The heavens grew dark
    With heavy rain
    Now
    Moving more rapidly
    Toward the Tree,
    Thunder boomed,
    Lightning exploded,
    Lighting
    The Valley of Oaxaca
    With
    A
    Bright blue light.

The Zapotec moved not a muscle
    Of his body.
    His jaw was set,
  His eyes reflecting
  The astonishment
  He felt.

From the bright spot on
       The Tree trunk
       Pockwatchies
       were coming.
       First one,
       Then more,
       A dozen of the little people
       coming fast,
       Followed by
       Even more,
       Singing as they came.
       They wore stars on their wrists
       And
       Carried God Eyes in their hands.
       Dancing in flight,
       They passed by the old man
       And
       He could hear their brave song,
       Never heard before,
       Not even
       By them.

"The Glory, The tree, of God, the hill
The Glory, the stream, the whippoorwill
The Glory, the wind, of God, the rain
The Glory, from clouds. the People came
The Glory, of God, is with us now
The Glory, of God, the sacred bough."

He watched as they poured
   from the Tree,
   By the hundreds,
   The thousands
   And
   Still more came,
   Leaping and gliding
   Whirling and springing again
   into the sky
   They traveled,
   Making a path of light
   Up toward the heavens.

   On they went, touching the heart
   Of every human on Earth,
   Touching their minds,
   Their souls
   With a new awareness
   A new glory.

   And the Earth Mother glowed with
   Happiness
   For she knew
   The Little People
   Were touching the
   Souls of men
   With a new magic power,
   A power never
   Completely
   Realized before,

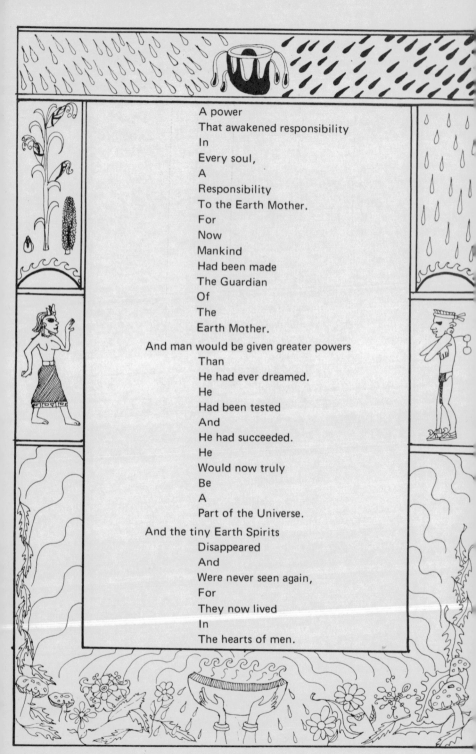

A power
That awakened responsibility
In
Every soul,
A
Responsibility
To the Earth Mother.
For
Now
Mankind
Had been made
The Guardian
Of
The
Earth Mother.

And man would be given greater powers
Than
He had ever dreamed.
He
Had been tested
And
He had succeeded.
He
Would now truly
Be
A
Part of the Universe.

And the tiny Earth Spirits
Disappeared
And
Were never seen again,
For
They now lived
In
The hearts of men.

"It is true!" said the Zapotec,

"Yes,

It is true,"

He stepped closer to

The huge Tree,

Much closer.

"The Glory of God is with us now

The Glory of God, the sacred bough . . ."

And

The Clouds

Drenched

The Earth

With

Love. . . . .

THE CLASSIFYING TERM FOR THIS CALENDAR IS "CUAUHXICALLI" (EAGLE'S BOWL), BUT IT IS UNIVERSALLY KNOWN AS THE AZTEC CALENDAR, OR SUN STONE, AS THE MONUMENT WAS DEDICATED TO THIS DEITY. ON THIS HUGE BASALTIC MONOLITH, HAVING AN APPROXIMATE WEIGHT OF 25 TONS, THE AZTEC CALENDAR WAS CARVED. IT WAS FOUND BURIED ON THE SOUTH-EAST CORNER OF THE ZOCALO (THE MAIN SQUARE) OF THE CITY OF MEXICO, ON DECEMBER 17TH, 1760. THE VICEROY OF THE NEW SPAIN AT THE TIME WAS DON JOAQUIN DE MONSERRAT, MARQUIS OF CRUILLAS. AFTERWARDS IT WAS TAKEN TO THE METROPOLITAN CATHEDRAL AND PLACED ON THE WEST WALL OF THE TOWER, WHERE IT REMAINED UNTIL THE YEAR OF 1885, WHEN PRESIDENT GENERAL PORFIRIO DIAZ ORDERED ITS TRANSFER TO THE NATIONAL MUSEUM OF ARCHAEOLOGY AND HISTORY. DURING THE REIGN OF THE 6TH AZTEC MONARCH, AXAYACATL, IT WAS THAT THIS STONE WAS CARVED AND DEDICATED TO THEIR PRINCIPAL DEITY, THE SUN, WHICH HAS BOTH A MYTHOLOGICAL AND ASTRONOMICAL CHARACTER.

OCELOTONATIUH
(SUN OF JAGUAR),
WAS THE "FIRST AND MOST REMOTE OF THE FOUR COSMOGONIC EPOCHS, IN WHICH THE GIANTS WHO HAD BEEN CREATED BY THE GODS, LIVED. THEY DID NOT TILL THE SOIL AND LIVED IN CAVES, ATE WILD FRUITS AND ROOTS, AND WERE FINALLY ATTACKED AND DEVOURED BY THE JAGUARS... THE BASIC EPOCH OF THE QUATERNARY, SINCE THEY DISCOVERED BONES OF PRE-DILUVIAN ANIMALS BURIED IN DEEP GULLIES BELOW DENSE LYTHOSPHERIC LAYERS.

TONATIUH'S FACE (THE FACE OF THE SUN) WHO WAS THE LORD OF HEAVEN, AROUND WHICH TOOK PLACE ALL DAILY OR PERIODIC PHENOMENA. THE CROWN, NOSE PENDANT, EAR-RINGS, AND NECKLACE, ARE MOST LUXURIOUS AND ARE THE ORNAMENTS PROPER OF THIS DEITY. THE HAIR WAS FAIR DUE TO THE GOLDEN APPEARANCE OF THE STAR, AND THE WRINKLES ON THE FACE WERE TO SHOW GREAT MATURITY OR AGE; AND THE TONGUE, LIKE AN OBSIDIAN KNIFE STUCK OUTWARD INDICATED THE NEED OF BEING FED WITH BLOOD AND HUMAN HEARTS.

PLATE OF THE CONSECRATION AN DEDICATION OF THIS STONE WITH THE DATE 13-ACATL (13-CANE) EQUIVALENT TO THE YEAR OF 1479 A.D.

THE ORNAMENTS OF CHALCHIHUITES (PRECIOUS) ARE MADE WITH JADE PLATES HAVING FIVE PERFORATIONS AND WERE ATTACHED BY MEANS OF RED LEATHER THONGS, AND FEATHER TIPS ENDING IN A PEARL. THIS IS THE MOST MAGNIFICENT ORNAMENT AND IT MEANS: LIGHT, STRENGTH AND BEAUTY.

THE "V" FIGURES ARE THE SIGNS OF SOLAR LIGHT BEAMS

THE DATE
1 - TECPATL
(1-OBSIDIAN KNIFE)
SYMBOL OF THE NORTH

THE TAIL OF THE XIUCOATL (FIRE SERPENT)

SYMBOLS OF SPLASHED BLOOD NOURISHING THE FLAMES AT THE BACK OF THE XIUCOATLS

THE SIGN XIUHUITZOLLI
(SYMBOLS OF THE EAST),
COAT OF ARMS WHICH WAS PLACED ON THE CORPSES OF THE NOBLEMEN AND BRAVE WARRIORS FOR THEIR FUNERALS

THE SIGN TLACHINOLLI (FLAMING SIGN) IN EACH OF THE SEGMENTS OF THE TWO XIUCOATLS (FIRE SERPENTS)

A BUNDLE OF HERBS WITH FLOWER BUDS

FOUR BOUND STRIPES OF AMATL (NATURAL PAPER) MADE OF AGAVE PLANT

EHECATONATIUH
(SUN OF WIND),
"SECOND EPOCH, AT THE END OF WHICH HUMANITY WAS DESTROYED BY STRONG WINDS
THE GODS TRANSFORMED HUMAN BEINGS INTO APES, IN ORDER THAT THEY MIGHT CLING BETTER AND NOT BE CARRIED AWAY BY THE HURRIACANES, THUS ORIGINATING THE SIMILARITY BETWEEN THE HUMAN RACE AND THE SIMIANS...
THIS WAS BECAUSE LARGE FORESTS HAD BEEN FOUND RAZED BY TORNADOES.

THE CLAWS OF THE SUN GOD, WITH WHICH IT IS SUPPOSED TO BE SUSPENDED IN SPACE; THEY HAVE A CHALCHIHUITE BRACELET, EYE AND EYE-BROW, AND A HUMAN HEART BETWEEN THE NAILS

ONE OF THE FOUR NUMERAL DOTS OF THE SIGN NAHUI-OLIN (SUN OF EARTHQUAKE)

20 TH DAY XOCHITL (FLOWER) LAST OF THE MONTH

19 TH DAY QUIAHUITL (RAIN)

18 TH DAY TECPATL (OBSIDIAN KNIFE)

17 TH DAY OLIN (EARTHQUAKE)

1 ST DAY CIPACTLI (CROCODILE)

2 ND DAY EHECATL (WIND)

3 RD DAY CALLI (HOUSE)

4 TH DAY CUETZPALLIN (LIZAR*)

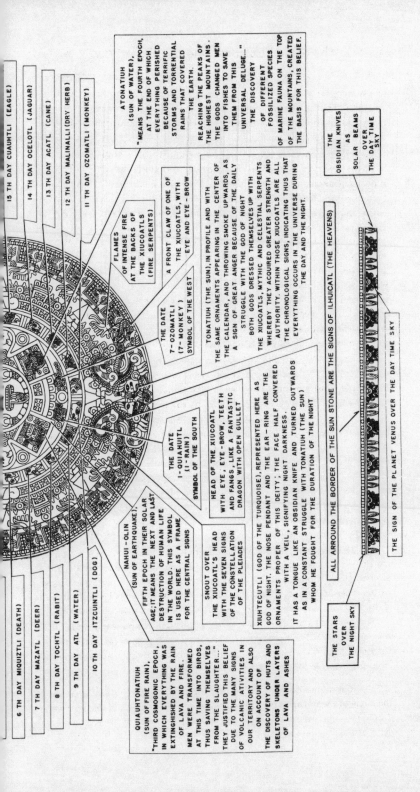

15 TH DAY CUAUHTLI (EAGLE)

14 TH DAY OCELOTL (JAGUAR)

13 TH DAY ACATL (CANE)

12 TH DAY MALINALLI (DRY HERB)

11 TH DAY OZOMATLI (MONKEY)

ATONATIUH
(SUN OF WATER),
"MEANS THE FOURTH EPOCH,
AT THE END OF WHICH
EVERYTHING PERISHED
BECAUSE OF TERRIFIC
STORMS AND TORRENTIAL
RAINS THAT COVERED
THE EARTH.
REACHING THE PEAKS OF
THE HIGHEST MOUNTAINS.
THE GODS CHANGED MEN
INTO FISHES TO SAVE
THEM FROM THIS
UNIVERSAL DELUGE..."
THE DISCOVERY
OF DIFFERENT
FOSSILIZED SPECIES
OF MARINE FAUNA ON THE TOP
OF THE MOUNTAINS, CREATED
THE BASIS FOR THIS BELIEF.

FLAMES
OF INTENSE FIRE
AT THE BACKS OF
THE XIUCOATLS
(FIRE SERPENTS)

THE DATE
7-OZOMATLI
(7-MONKEY)
SYMBOL OF THE WEST

A FRONT CLAW OF ONE OF
THE XIUCOATLS, WITH
EYE AND EYE-BROW

TONATIUH (THE SUN), IN PROFILE AND WITH
THE SAME ORNAMENTS APPEARING IN THE CENTER OF
THE CALENDAR, AND THROWING SMOKE UPWARDS, AS
A SIGN OF GREAT ANGER BECAUSE OF THE DAILY
STRUGGLE WITH THE GOD OF NIGHT
BOTH GODS DRESSED THEMSELVES UP WITH
THE XIUCOATLS, MYTHIC AND CELESTIAL SERPENTS
WHEREBY THEY ACQUIRED GREATER STRENGTH AND
AUTHORITY. WITHIN THOSE XIUCOATLS ARE ALL
THE CHRONOLOGICAL SIGNS, INDICATING THUS THAT
EVERYTHING OCCURS IN THE UNIVERSE DURING
THE DAY AND THE NIGHT.

THE
OBSIDIAN KNIVES
AS
SOLAR BEAMS
OVER
THE DAY TIME
SKY

THE DATE
1-QUIAHUITL
(1-RAIN)
SYMBOL OF THE SOUTH

HEAD OF THE XIUCOATL
WITH EYE, EYE-BROW, TEETH
AND FANGS, LIKE A FANTASTIC
DRAGON WITH OPEN GULLET

QUIAUHTONATIUH
(SUN OF FIRE RAIN),
"THIRD COSMOGONIC EPOCH,
IN WHICH EVERYTHING WAS
EXTINGUISHED BY THE RAIN
OF LAVA AND FIRE.
MEN WERE TRANSFORMED
AT THIS TIME INTO BIRDS,
THUS SAVING THEMSELVES
FROM THE SLAUGHTER..."
THEY JUSTIFIED THIS BELIEF
DUE TO THE MANY SIGNS
OF VOLCANIC ATIVITIES IN
OUR TERRITORY AND ALSO
ON ACCOUNT OF
THE DISCOVERY OF HUTS AND
SKELETONS UNDER LAYERS
OF LAVA AND ASHES

NAHUI-OLIN
(SUN OF EARTHQUAKE),
FIFTH EPOCH IN THEIR SOLAR
AGE, IT MEANS THE NEXT AND LAST
DESTRUCTION OF HUMAN LIFE
IN THE WORLD. THIS SYMBOL
IS USED HERE AS A FRAME
FOR THE CENTRAL SIGNS

SNOUT OVER
THE XIUCOATL'S HEAD
WITH THE SEVEN SIGNS
OF THE CONSTELLATION
OF THE PLEIADES

XIUHTECUTLI (GOD OF THE TURQUOISE), REPRESENTED HERE AS
GOD OF NIGHT. THE NOSE PENDANT AND THE EAR-RING ARE THE
ORNAMENTS PROPER OF THIS DEITY; THE FACE HALF CONVERED
WITH A VEIL, SIGNIFYING NIGHT DARKNESS.
IT HAS A TONGUE LIKE AN OBSIDIAN KNIFE AND TURNED OUTWARDS
AS IN A CONSTANT STRUGGLE WITH TONATIUH (THE SUN)
WHOM HE FOUGHT FOR THE DURATION OF THE NIGHT

6 TH DAY MIQUIZTLI (DEATH)

7 TH DAY MAZATL (DEER)

8 TH DAY TOCHTLI (RABIT)

9 TH DAY ATL (WATER)

10 TH DAY ITZCUINTLI (DOG)

ALL ARROUND THE BORDER OF THE SUN STONE ARE THE SIGNS OF ILHUICATL (THE HEAVENS)

THE SIGN OF THE PLANET VENUS OVER THE DAY TIME SKY

THE STARS
OVER
THE NIGHT SKY

Diagram II

The Sacred Calendar and the Eagle Bowl

Diagram I, page 192, is an explanation of the so-called Aztec Calendar. Its proper name is the Eagle Bowl, and it is a representation of the Aztec Sun God, Tonatiuh. The Eagle Bowl incorporates much of the mathematics and many of the glyphs of the Sacred Calendar of earlier cultures, and was by no means a creation of the Aztec Empire.

Seven hundred years before the birth of Christ a form of the calendar was in use in Vera Cruz, Mexico, at the ancient Olmec city of La Venta. At Monte Alban, in Oaxaca, a slightly different calendar was in use about the same time. Certain glyphs found on the Eagle Bowl are found in Tabasco and Yucatan where the Sacred Calendar was used almost 2,000 years before the Aztecs arrived in the Valley of Mexico.

In truth, the Sacred Calendar was used by all the inhabitants of Middle-America. The Aztec called it Tonalpohualli (the Book of Days), the Mayan knew it as Tzolkin (Wheel of the Days). To the Zapotec of Oaxaca, it was the Pije (Pije) and the Mixe called it Kuzhir (Keeper-of-the-Days). (Whatever it was called, its use was the same.) It worked like a horoscope at birth, and the child would be given his calendar name — 8 deer, 5 water, 1 reed, etc. The Sacred Calendar was also used to determine days of celebration, feast, and days to fast, lucky and unlucky days, and days of sacrifice to the gods.

The Sacred Calendar has 260 days in a year. The number 260 is arrived at by the use of 13 numbers and 20-day signs or glyphs, 13 x 20 equals 260. Diagram II illustrates how it worked. The same combination of glyph and number will not be repeated until 13 x 20 or 260 days had passed.

The 260-day calendar was also used as a 260-year cycle. If one examines this system closely, he will be quite amazed at the accuracy — 5 x 52 equals 260, 73 revolutions of the 260-day calendar equals 52 revolutions of the 365-day calendar. Actually there are 365¼ days in a solar year. We compensate for the one fourth day with a leap year. The Sacred Calendar saved the one-fourth day for 52 years and accumulated "13 days." A Mexican cycle was 52 solar years plus 13 days. Thus — each Heaven and each Hell of the prophecy is represented by a 52-year cycle, starting in 843 of our calendar. Thirteen cycles later, the thirteen Heavens were closed, in the year 1519 of our calendar.

The 260-day count, the Sacred Calendar of Middle-America, was a great deal more than a time counter. It was a way of life, a constant reminder of the ever-present gods. It predicted the future and recalled the past. It was perfect, as nature is perfect. It was an endless circle, without a real beginning and without a real end. In this way, it was a symbol of life, as the Indians believed it.

The center of the Eagle Bowl represents our sun (the present world). The four glyphs within the center circle represent four past worlds, each having been destroyed according to the tradition, and the date of the destruction is recorded "4 Wind, 4 Water, 4 Jaguar, and 4 Rain."

The four glyphs point in four different directions, forming a stylized cross, the circle of the universe, the cross of the winds. The circle and the cross were a universal sign among the American Indians, a symbol of life within a universe of life.

Pije
Translation
(Book of Days)

1. Cipactli (Alligator)	1	8	2	9	3	10	4	11	5	12	6	13	7
2. Ehecatl (Wind)	2	9	3	10	4	11	5	12	6	13	7	1	8
3. Calli (House)	3	10	4	11	5	12	6	13	7	1	8	2	9
4. Cuetzpallin (Lizard)	4	11	5	12	6	13	7	1	8	2	9	3	10
5. Coatl (Serpent)	5	12	6	13	7	1	8	2	9	3	10	4	11
6. Miquiztli (Death)	6	13	7	1	8	2	9	3	10	4	11	5	12
7. Mazatl (Deer)	7	1	8	2	9	3	10	4	11	5	12	6	13
8. Tochtli (Rabbit)	8	2	9	3	10	4	11	5	12	6	13	7	1
9. Atl (Water)	9	3	10	4	11	5	12	6	13	7	1	8	2
10. Itzcuintli (Dog)	10	4	11	5	12	6	13	7	1	8	2	9	3
11. Ozomatli (Monkey)	11	5	12	6	13	7	1	8	2	9	3	10	4
12. Malinalli (Grass)	12	6	13	7	1	8	2	9	3	10	4	11	5
13. Acatl (Reed)	13	7	1	8	2	9	3	10	4	11	5	12	6
14. Ocelotl (Jaguar)	1	8	2	9	3	10	4	11	5	12	6	13	7
15. Cuauhtli (Eagle)	2	9	3	10	4	11	5	12	6	13	7	1	8
16. Cozcacuauhtli (Buzzard)	3	10	4	11	5	12	6	13	7	1	8	2	9
17. Ollin (Earthquake)	4	11	5	12	6	13	7	1	8	2	9	3	10
18. Tecpatl Flint Knife)	5	12	6	13	7	1	8	2	9	3	10	4	11
19. Quiahuitl (Rain)	6	13	7	1	8	2	9	3	10	4	11	5	12
20. Xochitl (Flower)	7	1	8	2	9	3	10	4	11	5	12	6	13

Diagram I

To The Reader

Assuming you have read "Lord of the Dawn," and hoping that you have thought about it, you now realize it is not like other books about Ancient Mexico, in fact it is not much like any other book you have ever read.

If you are a scholar of Pre-Columbian history you are no doubt scratching your head and wondering what I'm up to.

If on the other hand you are a newcomer to "all this" you are no doubt wondering why you have not heard of it before, and where you may learn more about it.

There is a great deal more to say about the Thirteen Heavens and the Nine Hells. There is more to say about the death of Ce Acatl Topiltzin, about his tomb, about his philosophy, about his prayers and about his followers. All of that will come in due time. But those things are not the next step in understanding these concepts.

One success of "Lord of the Dawn", serving its purpose, will appear in the desire of the reader to absorb all available materials on the subject of Pre-Columbian history and actual Indian ceremony. To aid in this pursuit we have supplied a "Recommended Book List" of writings by scholars and scientists who are regarded as authorities in the field of American Anthropology.

Ce Acatl Topiltzin said: *"You will not know me by my miracles. You will know me by the 'Tree'. . . .But, we WILL do miracles."*

If one pursues that thought through Indian religion and ceremony he will certainly find that the heart of Indian religion is the "Tree."

Other books about ancient Mexico declare the "Lord of the Dawn" is dead. This book claims that is not true. It says He is not done with all of this, not yet. His voice trumpets out of Mexico's past, it is sung by the Chicanos, Mexican Americans, Mexican Indians. It booms like the beat of a thousand drums across this land. Sioux, Cheyenne, Cherokee, Pueblo. . . .the pure bloods, Black and Indian, Irish Indian, Scotch, Dutch and English Indian -- all nationalities are touched with Indian blood and the dreams of the "Old Way." Dreams of equality of the races, rights of women, rights of the individual to remain an individual, rights to pursue God in our own way, world unity, peace, freedom and the God-given rights to live life as each one feels it. The philosophy of Quetzalcoatl shall be done on Earth.

Today as never before in the history of mankind we are faced with the frightening problem of pollution. We, in America have coined the word "ecology" as the study of that problem, just as "religion" is the word for the concept of God. If future generations are to survive on this planet, mankind throughout the world must come to accept the fact that this Earth is a living thing, with spirit and feelings not much different from our own spirit and our own feelings. We must teach our children at home and in school that the Earth is, in fact, our Mother and she must be respected and cared for. We must teach our children that the spirit of this planet in our time is exemplified by mankind. And that when a river, lake, forest or field, city or seashore dies it is because of man's lack of concern for accepting the spiritual responsibility of the Earth Mother.

Mankind today has the ability to change the course of history. The question is, does he realize he must submit to God, in order to do it right?

(Note: a companion volume of this book is in preparation, called THE BOY AND THE TREE.)

Books About Pre-Columbian History

Ancient Oaxaca. Edited by John Paddock, with contributions by Ignacio Bernal, Alfonso Caso, Robert Chadwick, Howard F. Cline, Wigberto Jimenez Moreno, Howard Leigh, John Paddock, Donald Robertson and Charles R. Wicke. Stanford University Press. 1966.

AZTEC - People of the Sun. By Alfonso Caso. Illustrated by Miguel Covarrubias. University of Oklahoma Press. Norman, Oklahoma. 1967.

Burning Water - Thought and Religion in Ancient Mexico. By Laurette Sejourne. Vanguard Press.

Indian Art of Mexico and Central America. By Miguel Covarrubias. Published by Alfred A. Knopf. New York. 1957.

Mexico South - The Isthmus of Tehuantepec. By Miguel Covarrubias. Published by Alfred A. Knopf. New York. 1964.

Plumed Serpent - (a novel). By D. H. Lawrence. Published by Alfred A. Knopf. New York. 1951.

Popol Vuh - Sacred Book of the Ancient Quiche Maya. By Recinos, Coetz, Morley. University of Oklahoma Press. 1969.

Zapotec. By Helen Augur. (out of print).

Books Related to subject matter of Lord of the Dawn

Gleanings from the Writings of Baha'u'llah. Translated by Shoghi Effendi. Baha'i Publishing Committee, Wilmette, Illinois.

Book of the Hopi. By Frank Waters and Oswald White Bear Fredericks. Viking Press and Ballantine Books. 1963.

Gospel of the Redman. By Ernest Thompson Seton. Boy Scouts of America. 1971.

Masked Gods. By Frank Waters. Swallow Press and Ballantine Books. New York.

Sacred Pipe - Black Elk's Account of the Seven Rites of the Oglala Sioux. Recorded and Edited by Joseph Epes Brown. University of Oklahoma Press. Norman, Oklahoma. 1968.

Tapestries in Sand. By David Villasenor. Naturegraph Publishers, Healdsburg, California. 1966.

Warriors of the Rainbow. By William Willoya and Vinson Brown. Naturegraph Publishers, Healdsburg, California. 1962.

Way to Rainy Mountain. By Scott Momaday. University of New Mexico Press. 1970.

Pronunciation Glossary

Amanteca *(A - maan - Tay - ca)*
Master builders of the Toltec City of Tollan.

Ce Acatl Topiltzin *(Say - A - cattle To - pilt - zin)*
One Reed — Our Lord.

Chapultepec *(Cha - pool - ta - pec)*
Grasshopper Hill in present day Mexico City.

Chimalma *(Cha - Mal - ma)*
The incarnation of the Goddess of Flowers and Love. The earth mother of the Lord of the Dawn.

Chichen - Itza *(Chee - chan - Et - za)*
Twin city of Tollan, located in Yucatan. Originally a Mayan city, rebuilt by Toltec-Mayan after 1000 A. D.

Chichimeca *(Chee - che - me - Ka)*
"People of Dog Lineage." Nomad invaders of the Valley of Mexico.

Chilam Balam *(Chee - lam Bah - lam)*
Mayan priest who wrote prophetic books about 1500 A. D.

Cholula *(Cho - Lu - la)*
Site of the largest Pyramid in the Americas. Located near Puebla, Mexico.

Cosijo *(Koh - see - hoh)*
Zapotec name for the rain god. Tlaloc was the name used in the Valley of Mexico.

Deganaweda *(Day - gan - a - we - dah)*
Iroquois prophet born in 1571.

Gucumatz *(Wah - Ku - Mat - s)*
Disciple of Ce Acatl, and the one who became the Mayan Indian Lord.

HiKuli *(I - Ku - lee)*
Name applied to sacred Peyote cactus. Used as a sacrament by many Indians of Mexico. Called Father Peyote of the Native American Church.

Huichol *(Whee - chol)*
Tribe of Indians living in the state of Nayarit, Mexico. Called the "Happy People."

Huiteca *(whesh - teca)*
Tribe of Indians. Neighbor of the Zapotec.

Kukulcan *(Ku - Kul - Kan)*
Mayan name for the Plumed Serpent — (Quetzalcoatl).

Mazatec *(Mah - zah - tec)*
Tribe of Indians in Oaxaca.

Mitla *(Meet - lah)*
Ancient Religious center of the Indians of Oaxaca, a sort of Vatican of America. Designed by the Lord of the Dawn.

Mixcoatl *(Mish - Co - atl)*
Leader of the Chichimeca, father of Lord of the Dawn. Mixcoatl, Sky Serpent, Milky Way, and Tree of the Sky.

Nahuatl *(Na - Wah - tl)*
Linguistic group—Chichimec, Toltec, Aztec and many other people still speak Nahuatl.

Pronunciation Glossary

Nonoalca *(No - No - al - ka)*
Priestly followers of Lord of the Dawn. Builders of the city Tollan.

Oaxaca *(Wah - Hah - Kah)*
Southern state in the Republic of Mexico.

Peyote *(Pay - o - tee)*
Hallucinogenic cactus, a sacrament of the Native American Church of the U.S.

Popocatepetl *(Poh - Poh - cat - a - petl)*
Volcano east of Mexico City.

Quetzal *(Kwet - zahl)* or *(Ket - sal)*
A Central American bird with golden green and scarlet feathers.

Quetzalcoatl *(Kwet - zal - coh - ahtl)* or *(Ket - sal - Ko - a - tl)*
Feathered Serpent God of Ancient Mexico. Incarnated as a man in 947 A. D., "Lord of the Dawn."

Quiche Mayan *(Ke - cha)*
Indian language of Guatemala.

Quill *(Ko - will)*
Pockwatchie Lord, ruler of the "Navel of the Earth", master of games and fish.

Tehuantepec *(Tay - hooan - Tay - Peck)*
Isthmus of Southern Mexico. Also Castulo Romero's hometown.

Tenochtitlan *(Ten - oak - teet - LAHN)*
Capital city of the Aztec at the time of the Conquest of Mexico.

Teotihuacan *(Tay - oh - tee - whah - Kahn)*
"City of the Gods." 21 miles north of Mexico City. Site of the Pyramids of the sun and of the moon.

Tezcatlipoca *(Tes - cat - lee - po - Ka)*
Black god of the north. Smoking Mirror, ruler of the past world. Quetzalcoatl's brother.

Lake Tezcoco *(Tesh - co - co)*
The lake which now lies under Mexico City.

Tlaloc *(Tla - lok)*
The rain-god of the Valley of Mexico.

Tlaloque *(Tla - loo - Kee)*
Servant of the rain-god Tlaloc, guardian of the Earth Mother. Never more than two inches tall, extremely powerful, capable of causing lightning and bringing rain.

Tollan *(Toll - lahn)*
City of the Toltec or place of the Toltec. Located a few miles from the present city of Tula.

Xochicalco *(sho - She - cal - Ko)*
City of the Feathered Serpent, located south of Mexico City.

Zapotec *(Sap - o - tec)*
Important Indian language spoken in the state of Oaxaca, Mexico. The name Zapotec is from the Aztec; the Zapotec's name for themselves is Ben-Zaa.

An Interpretation Of The Cover Drawing

Once the Sacred Tree was beautiful, limbs and branches filled with living leaves of silver and jade. Now it is all but gone. Symbolizing the Tree of Ancient America, her roots plunge downward into the Earth Mother and grip the forgotten past. Tears flow from the straining earth as if she would sacrifice anything to bring the tree back to life and beauty.

Behind the Tree to the left is the Sacred Mountain. All great peoples of the earth have had such mountains, each a place to meditate, to commune with the Spirit, to fast and pray.

The Indian rises up from the waters holding a green bough in his hands so that his words shall be living words of truth and spirit. But behind him is the shattering frightful world of today, filled with disharmony. Two perfect spheres are visible through the turmoil, one symbolizing the male, the other the female principle, negative and positive, God and Man.

Above, in a scene of storm, the Lord of the Dawn peers down over the frustrations of the earth. As a representative of the Great Spirit he is above all pettiness of race or nationality, yet he is undoubtedly an Indian, bearded as some Indians are.

On the right side of the picture the world appears in peace. The rainbow bridges the horizon of a new dawn, connecting the Tree with "something" outside of the picture. And the Morning Star dominates the sky with the Promise of a Glorious New Sunrise.